Harold Finch-Hatton

Voices Through Many Years

Vol. I

Harold Finch-Hatton

Voices Through Many Years
Vol. I

ISBN/EAN: 9783744752916

Printed in Europe, USA, Canada, Australia, Japan

Cover: Foto ©ninafisch / pixelio.de

More available books at **www.hansebooks.com**

VOICES
THROUGH MANY YEARS.

BY

GEORGE JAMES

EARL OF WINCHILSEA AND NOTTINGHAM

(VISCOUNT MAIDSTONE).

VOL. I.

'Nonumque prematur in annum,
Membranis intus positis.'
HORACE, *Ars Poetica*, line 388-9.

Printed for Private Circulation only.

LONDON:

MARCUS WARD & CO. 67 CHANDOS STREET.

M.DCCC.LXXIX.

CONTENTS OF VOL. I.

Dedication.

TO

THE RIGHT HON. GEORGE, EARL OF STRAFFORD.

'Strafford the polite,
And gentle Osborne told me I could write.'
POPE—*in a new suit.*

MY DEAR STRAFFORD,

You have permitted me to dedicate to you these fugitive pieces which have now reached over so many years. This, I expected of your friendship, for when I first began to write, you encourag'd me, and it is but fair that you should accept a share of the responsibility.

There is yet another friend whose memory is dear to both of us, the gentle LORD SYDNEY OSBORNE, who agreed with you in wishing success to the muse of JOHN DAVIS. I have join'd his name with yours in the lines that I have altered from Pope's 'Essay on Criticism.'

As many of the allusions are no longer matters of notoriety, I have added as many dates and notes as I think are necessary to explain them.

'Voices through many years' were written as occasion suggested; and it will therefore be intelligible to many of my friends whose politics are of a different order, that some things contain'd in them will not be to their taste; but I hope they will forgive me on the ground that the essence of politics is to give and receive shrewd hits: and no one in his time has receiv'd more, than

Your friend and well-wisher,

WINCHILSEA AND NOTTINGHAM.

VOICES THROUGH MANY YEARS.

The Fountain of Trevi.

FEB. 14TH, 1837. (*Published in the 'Keepsake.'*)

'C'est le bruit des voitures que l'on a besoin d'entendre dans les autres villes. C'est le murmure de cette fontaine immense qui semble comme l'accompagnement nécessaire à l'existence reveuse qu'on y mene.'

CORINNE (*end of Fourth Book*).

THE din of day was hush'd and o'er,
The wranglers for gain were heard no more.
Each had departed—a little while
To taste repose from a life of toil;
But a tumult reigned in my fev'r'd breast,
It could not, would not, might not rest.

Ev'ry charm that once had pleas'd
Pall'd upon a mind diseas'd;
Pen and pencil, friend and book,
Each were tried, and each forsook.

A hurried mixture of pleasure and pain
Thrill'd in gusts athwart my brain.
I could not bear my thoughts at home;
So I wander'd forth through the streets of Rome.

Gasping the night breeze to cool the flame
That lit my heart to its inmost frame,
With hurried pace I strode on still,
Stifling thoughts for good and ill.
Threading many a narrow way,
Where the robber lurks for his heedless prey;
Little reck'd I of him that day.
But now the balm of a chilling sky
Had work'd, in part, a remedy;
I look'd to Heaven, I look'd to earth,
I felt as if new thoughts had birth;—
Till at length, reliev'd from misery,
The soul on her course sped tranquilly.

Then I thought as I walk'd the spot,
Where yet stands Rome though Rome is not,
There must be spirits slumb'ring here,
(Like the murder'd slave of the buccaneer,)
To weep for her they can't defend,
To be, as once in life, her friend.

Ye, iron hearts of Brutus' mould,
Ye 'Scipios' and 'Camillus'' old!
How do your mighty deeds remain;
Yourselves in memory live again.
What!—Though your offspring be debas'd,
Your 'stamp' be from their minds eras'd?

Yet still, ye are not childless all!
Nor shall be—while one patriot soul
Beat, as he turns with rapt'rous hand
The page no slave may understand;
To draw from it the lesson stern
That Freedom's sons shall love to learn:—
How to deserve, and win, and hold
The prize for which ye strove of old.
These are the children ye shall find,
Not of the lineage, but the mind!
This is the offspring ye may own
In ev'ry clime, from ev'ry zone!
Oh! could ye but instil a flame
In Romans—(Romans but in name,)
Then would their hands be readier far
Than now their tongues in wordy war!
The patriot's spear and biting blade
Should carve a bitterer Pasquinade
Than e'er in nameless mock'ry rear'd,
On 'Ajax' crumbling form appear'd!

Thus musing, still I wander'd on
In converse with the dead and gone.
Through many a freakish turn pursued
The prompting of my wayward mood,
Till full express'd against the sky
'The Trevi' rose to meet mine eye.

It was, as I have said, a night
Congenial to the restless sprite!
The air was chill, the winds were low,
And little clouds would come and go.

The Moon in southern lustre shone,
Pointing with light each hoary stone;
Each rugged limb of the giants old
That watch'd the water as it roll'd.
I sat me down by the dark pool's brim,
And gaz'd on the spray till mine eyes grew dim;
Till—as by wand of magic art
From forth it—visions seem'd to start.

That solitude is doubly drear
Where mirth was wont to strike the ear!
'Tis in this spot that Traffic's sound
Dins through the day's unceasing round.
But then 'twas wrapp'd in silence all,
Like a corse that is wound in its funeral pall!
Silent and sad though now they lie,
Each shall be stirring by-and-by!
This at the dawn of to-morrow's sun,
That when the course of Time is run!

Nothing was heard at that lonely hour
But the bell that toll'd from some ancient tower;
Save, here and there, a patt'ring sound
Of foot-fall striking on the ground.
Nought else betoken'd living wight:
Such is Rome at dead of night.

Methought the moonbeams had express'd
A circle of haze on the fountain's breast;
And I felt compell'd to gaze thereon
By some strong Power I could not shun.

I knew that I stood in a stranger spot—
A foreign land that own'd me not;
Far from my country, friends, and all
That Mem'ry's visions would recall;
And I felt th' emotions—that thrilling come
O'er the bursting heart—when we think of home.

I mus'd on the days I had pass'd with thee
In mild delights and childish glee;
And how, sweet sister of my heart,
Thou and I from hence must part!
The love that bound us shall remain!
But hence, our home is not the same.
I thought of her who gave me birth,
Who usher'd me into the tumult of Earth;
And how she droop'd on a fatal day,
Suddenly, fearfully, summon'd away.
Her form before my mem'ry pass'd,
As on earth I saw it last;
I bent again o'er the open bier,
And gaz'd on her—my mother dear.
They were the features I ever knew;
Death had but stamp'd a paler hue;
But a waxen softness there was there,
For life too sad, and yet too fair;—
A sickly freshness creeping forth
Told the return of 'earth to earth;'
And shuddering I held my breath;—
For yet I had not look'd on Death!
I thought of days in pleasure pass'd,
In reckless mirth that cannot last;

And felt—the mind is made to be
Dependent much on sympathy:
That Love will soothe our varying strife
In the hurried round of human life.—
Ever and anon in my heated trance,
Of a 'peerless form' would I catch a glance.—
The flick'ring moonbeams shed a light
On the transient form of the lovely sprite.
The ripp'ling waters' drowsy fall,
Replied in accents musical;
I drank large draughts of sweet illusion
Deeply, to my soul's confusion.
When a shiv'ring start came o'er my brow;—
And the delicate vision had vanish'd now!

Feign would I then have homeward turn'd
To marshal forth again,
These images by fancy rais'd
Of pleasure and of pain;
But yet I cast mine eyes around
In philosophic mood,
And gazing on the costly pile
I linger'd where I stood.
There, had the Sculptor's art pourtray'd
The monarch of the Sea,
Just ris'n from his coral caves
In Ocean majesty;
Two Tritons curb'd his neighing steeds—
The 'trident' in his hand,
And from the rock un-number'd streams
Gush'd forth at his command.

But higher still I cast mine eyes
And there I might discern,—
(Engraven in high-sounding phrase,
For all to see and learn,)
A Legend of his name and style,
And when he fill'd his throne,
The Pope by whose munificence
This water ran in stone.

I gaz'd until in scornful mood
I could not but exclaim,
'What will not man's vain-glory work
To make himself a name?'
Yes!—so it is!—with mortal men!
Selfish they still remain!
One plants and toils to place the seed,
Another reaps the grain!
And for themselves insatiably
The great all honours claim;—
Why find we not the well-earn'd scroll
That tells the sculptor's name?
And what care they who here resort
To quaff the waters thou hast brought,
So they but get the thing they need—
For thee and thine? Is this thy meed?
The honours of philanthropy—
The Fame for which 'twere cheap to die?

Yet in this Fountain's ceaseless flow
Is moral for the wise to know.
On, on we rush,—a stream of men,—
Falling and filling fast again.

To some their course is giv'n from high,
With noisy splash they hurry by;
Some drop in placid dignity,—
Some gently trickle down to die.
Yet—each and all at last must fall
Into that dark receptacle.
That murky gulf at last must hold
The timid, and the rashly bold!
The heart whose ev'ry pulse beat high,
Ecstatic all with Poesy;
And him—that clod of meagre clay
Who lives but for the passing day;
Nor feels one pulse of nobler mind
Than grovels in the bestial kind!

Yet still—though standing on the brink
Of Death's drear stream,—not all shall sink!
Dark as the yawning gulf appears,
Hopeless beyond our worst of fears;
On its foul bosom flits a gleam,
The Angel Hope's refreshing beam,
That says—'Although necessity
Proclaim the law that all must die,
Yet shall not all eternally.'

The musing Spirit left my soul,
A weight from off it seem'd to roll.
I felt relief;—and yet with pain
I turn'd me back to life again.

England's Worthies.

WRITTEN IN THE YEAR 1857.

BROTHER ENGLISHMAN! bethink thee ever who and what thou art!
Of what great and glorious Empire thou—the least one—mak'st a part!
Brother Englishman, bethink thee, somewhat of this potent whole
Is entrusted to thy keeping,—rests within thy life's control.
Wheresoever morning find thee, in whatever hemisphere,
Let thy deeds be more than Roman, and thy conscience ever clear!
Wheresoever evening leave thee—recollect! thy Country's fame
Glows with individual honour, pales with individual shame.
Shiv'ring in the snows of 'Zembla,' wrestling with the gales of 'Horn,'
Fost'ring commerce, founding empires, do no wrong! but brook no scorn!
Spare the vanquish'd! crush the tyrant! beat all opposition down!
Plan with cunning, strike with courage! Halt not on this side Renown!
Be more Spartan than 'Lycurgus!' suddener than 'Ammon's son!'
Wilier than the bald first 'Cæsar,' greater than 'Napoleon!'
More self-confident than 'Colon,' closer in thy purpose stern
Than the stumbling-block of 'Philip'—'William,' hight 'the Taciturn!'

Builder of enlightened progress! other conquerors than thee
(Pests appointed to the nations), have usurped the land and sea;
But since Rome's undying footprints, none hath left enduring trace!
Force may scatter—Legions ruin—wisdom only can replace!

Deep and prudent forethought only can root out the thing accurs'd,
And build up the 'Second Temple' in more honour than the 'first.'

Look upon the wondrous fabric! all 'the scarlet' maps contain;
All the vast possessions scattered o'er the mainland and the main!
Where on the behalf of progress, for the welfare of the world,
In the cause of genuine freedom, Britain's banner floats unfurl'd.
Is it by thy store of soldiers? never equall'd though they be;
Is it by thy jealous system of suspicious tyranny?
Is it by the gathering thunder of thy native hearts of oak?
Is it by the lightning swiftness of thy never-failing stroke?
Is it by thy prudent counsels? that in either hemisphere,
Such a motley swarm of nations rank'd around thy throne appear?
Is it by thy valour only? of all these enough we've heard!—
No!—'Tis by the blameless honour of thy never-broken word!
No!—'Perfidious' let them call thee, who have sought—thank Heaven, in vain!
To find profit in thy downfall, and in thy disaster gain!
This reproach will not be dealt thee by the later unborn age;
This will hardly be the verdict of judicious Hist'ry's page!

These will say, When 'Great Assyria' had been reap'd and laid away;
'Greece' and iron 'Rome' had fallen, windfalls of their own decay;
When the 'North' had wasted Europe, and the Spaniard had enchain'd
In a bond of tenfold darkness the New World which 'Colon' gain'd;
Then arose a mighty People! wiser, stronger than them all;
Borne to be the scourge of tyrants—and the saviour of the thrall!—

Hurrying on the car of progress over land and over sea;
By the steamship and the railroad, in unbeaten paths mov'd she!

All her sons were born for empire, with the habit of command!
Yet she was as widely famous for the inventive head and hand.
From her seat amidst the currents of old Ocean's wildest tides,
From her cliffs where Winter lingers, and ungenial mist abides,
Came in quick succession—victors over customs, men, and things;
Citizens whose deeds exceeded all that has been told of kings.

Foster'd by a race of monarchs, bluff and proud, and high of hand,
In great heart, but slow to ripen, grew the staple of this land:
Boldness, independence, freedom, never tiring energy,
Patience, cool resource in peril, courage—if need were—to die!
These produced the men of 'Crécy,' these upheld 'Black Edward' when
He pluck'd 'King John' from his war-horse, or kept holiday in 'Guienne.'
These supplied the stubborn archers that with 'Harry' turn'd to bay
'Gainst the chivalry of Gallia on Saint Crispin's famous day;
These sent 'Good Queen Bess,' in peril, soldiers true and sailors good;
Nobles, sages, knights, and yeomen, that could never be withstood,
When that high and valiant Princess cast in 'Philip's' teeth her glove,
And girt on her armour, trusting to a gen'rous people's love.

And there hung in rich profusion acorns on this grand oak-tree,
Such as never were aforetime, nor in after days shall be.
'Drake,' the impetuous, hardy sailor; 'Raleigh,' tender, active, true,
Plaything of the strangest fortunes, ever daring something new.
More adventurous than 'Arthur's' champions of the 'Table Round,'
None so learned, none so gallant, none so various and profound.
'Cromwell,' stern, unflinching, prudent, with whose deeds the world yet rings;—
Trampling with the heel of 'Joshua' on the dusty necks of kings.

Shackled by no tender conscience, master of the ways of man;
Policy, and arms, and commerce, parts of his majestic plan.
Most unlike those fickle Stuarts that no exile could reclaim :—
Jealous to the death of England's world-wide honour and good name.
'Blake,' the prototype of 'Nelson,' ready, sudden, patient, brave;
Dying like an ancient Sea-king, in his good ship on the wave.
'Penn,' and those self-exiled fathers that, with freedom for their guide,
Left their homes in 'Merrie England' for such cheer as woods provide:
Seeking there th' untrammelled worship that a Christian owes to God;
These endowed an 'unborn Giant' with the lands where 'Red Men' trod.

Statesmen, too, were never wanting, nor free men to lift their voice
'Gainst the spoilers of the People, worthy of the People's choice.
'Hampden's' name is not forgotten,—Chatham's thunder echoes still,
When he shook the thrones of Europe in the fury of his will.
'Walpole's' skill and subtle tactics and his glorious common-sense,
Fix'd a crown that might have fallen, but for him, on light pretence.
'Pit' and 'Fox's' stern encounters, battling o'er the Commonweal,
Live to be for aye remember'd with the wise career of Peel.

From what stock, however valiant, came in any age or time
Captains of more splendid fortunes, or of genius more sublime?
'Marlborough's' wars are still the model for a speculative mind,
Scheming what the sword can compass with just policy combin'd.
Strange that such a daring couple as 'Queen Sarah' and her man,
Should have nourish'd into glory the tea-table reign of Anne.

Young, unpromising, rebellious, by the hand of Fate consign'd,
In a weighty day for England, to the golden shores of Ind,
Came a petty clerk—to sum up ledgers in the factory,
To waste life on sordid figures, and without a name to die;—

But what soul can fathom fortune? who shall say which plants will
thrive?
Young, unpromising, rebellious, that immortal clerk was Clive!
Born a warrior without schooling, and a statesman, what lack'd he?
Nothing but what many pine for—happy opportunity.
And it came!—and like the comet, bursting into sudden blaze,
He left 'Timur-leng' behind him, and all Europe in amaze.
Almost ere the news could reach her, he had driven home the blow;
Riveting the 'Mongul's' shackles, baffling the Gallic foe.
Wild and wond'rous times before him, much to guess at, more to fear;
What upheld this empire-builder? Courage high, and genius clear.
And ere many have bethought them for what purpose life is lent,
He had conquer'd and established all that 'Alexander' meant!
Then returning to his country, from a more supreme command
Than had ever been allotted to the greatest subject's hand,
Butt for all the shafts of hatred, target of each envious tongue,
In the vale where Severn wanders his embow'ring woods among;
From the trickeries of state-craft and vicissitudes of strife,
Greater than he was in India—he retir'd to private life.

All majestic though his genius, England yet has given birth
To the equal of his fortunes, and a greater far in worth:
He too leaving Europe early, sought in Oriental strife
Heroes worthy of his mettle, fields now glorious by his life.
There he studied war and tactics,—'common sense' he called them aye,
And oppos'd to famous 'Plassy' the new wonders of 'Assaye.'
To return in time for England, and like 'Fabius' by delay
Reassure her hold on 'Fortune' that ne'er left him for a day!
Simple, energetic, prudent, fully conversant with men,
Fighting with the sword of Cæsar, making sure with Cæsar's pen.

Not like 'Marlborough' avaricious, not like 'Clive' unscrupulous, he
Never left a blot unpunish'd, but he fought with majesty.
And without parade a victor he observ'd the Roman law,
'Spar'd the vanquish'd, crush'd the tyrant,'—mingling courtesy with war.
Peace could not abate his prudence, nor surprise him into sleep,
And his voice was rais'd in warning, and it echoed wide and deep;
And it woke the 'seven sleepers' with the clarion notes of truth;—
In his latter days a 'watchman,' as a 'saviour' in his youth.
Still his ashes rest among us by the side of Nelson's laid;
Two such urns, sure, never rested in a single cloister's shade.
Then let all that bend in homage over Arthur Wellesley's dust
Say, 'Here rests a thorough soldier! Just, if ever man was just!'

Thron'd amid contending currents, that like horses issue forth
Harness'd to the car of whirlwinds, from the chambers of the North,
Colonis'd of ancient 'Vikings,' skimmers of the Frozen Seas,
Lords of every Southern sea-board; sons of battle, toil, and breeze;
It was meet that 'Merrie England' should have mariners in store
Such as never were aforetime in the vaunted days of yore!
More fool-hardy than the seekers for the fabled golden fleece,
Sweeping seas unknown to Carthage, undisturb'd by keels of Greece,
Love of peril and adventure, thirst for glory, lust of gain
Made them patriots in the Channel, pirates on the Spanish main;
Till the 'buccaneers' of 'Raleigh,' and 'Drake's' 'roving blades,' gave way
To the slowly-dawning promise of a less terrific day;
And the spirit of 'the Rover' a more genial aspect took;
Settling down in Anson's voyages, and the mild career of 'Cook.'
Then arose the greatest master of Britannia's special pride,
'The Leviathans of Ocean' on her subject floods that ride;

'Nelson,' of our isle the glory—none so far from 'self' remov'd;
He alone of all our worthies is, in troth, the man belov'd!
Darling of our fancy's childhood! Wonder of our manhood's prime!
In thy vigilance unequalled, in thy simple faith sublime!
Better sailor, humbler Christian, quarter-deck, sure, never trod,
With a more sublime reliance on the present hand of God.
Duty to thy king and country was thy leading star of life!
This upheld thy soul in sickness, this sustained thee in the strife!
And thy death, that bitter portion of Heaven's ministerial plan,
Bow'd the mighty heart of England as the spirit of one man!

Hand in hand with all these triumphs, ev'ry weapon born to wield,
Came philosophers, as daring as her soldiers in the field.
'Bacon,' whose plain common-dealing flung the logic of the schools
To the rubbish-basket—freeing all mankind from barren rules.
Pioneer of all the inventions,—all the plans with progress rife
To assist man's weary labour,—and make bearable his life.
'Milton,' patriot and poet, rapt into sublimer thought
Than, in the long roll of ages, uninspired Muse e'er taught.
'Newton'—Shakspeare the melodious, vers'd in madness, wit, and love;
Hundred-handed as 'Briareus' joining high debate with Jove.
'Glorious John' like 'Pindar' headlong,—'Byron' moodiest of his kind;
Greatest too,—a scoffing Titan,—poet of an ill-starr'd mind.

Sturdy sons of homelier fortunes in the due time came as well!
Usefuller, if not as brilliant, 'Arkwright,' 'Davy,' 'Watt,' Brunel.'
Who shall say what store of honey their benignant lives set free;
What new flowers their hand presented to the humble working bee?
What unheard-of powers of Nature liberated by their aid,
Came to bless alike the palace, and the wayside cabin's shade?

Then, with all these names before thee, these records of good and great;
Men that have brought help in peril or done service to the State;
On the muster-roll of Glory foremost of so many lands;
Workers with their swords and sinews, with their reason and their hands.
Some by birth ordain'd to govern as the Leaders of Mankind;
Most that have won Honour's chaplet by their inborn strength of mind;
With the records of their greatness cropping up on ev'ry hand,
Wafted back from ev'ry Ocean to one common Father-Land;
Laws, and Liberty, and Empire, Arts, and Arms, and Nature's spoil,
Portions of the stately fabric garnish'd by their general toil;—
'Brother Englishman' bethink thee, ever—who and what thou art!
Of what great and glorious Nation, thou, the least one, mak'st a part.

A Debate in the Olden Time.

A DIALOGUE. WRITTEN 1840.

MARGEITES.

Is it for this—men largely cringe and flatter,
And lick the scrapings of the public platter?
Vend their paternal acres,—spend their guineas,—
And raise themselves to highest rank,—(as ninnies?—)
To yawn—or make the House yawn in debate,
To frank a letter—(art defunct of late,)
To see odd sirnames lengthen'd by M.P.
And made still more untuneable,—to be
Pictures in little of the Public wit,
Nest-eggs on which Constituencies sit?
No! 'tis the Member's sense of 'public duty,'
That makes him wreak his talents on the Country;
That keeps Constituents' throats for ever dry;
And makes Election bribes in volleys fly;
Or does some thrifty Patriot seek to please;
He promises the knaves, the rich man's keys! . . .

CYMON.

Margeites, you are hard on public men!

MARGEITES.

Well, hear me out, thou simple sire! and then
Judge for thyself! 'The time of day is 'Four!''
Revolves 'St. Stephen's' Senatorial door,

And 'business men' by 'twos and threes' arrive:—
A hundred truants rush in just at 'five,'
And scramble headlong for a vacant seat,
And brush the dusty floor with dustier feet,
And play the Devil—rustle, squeeze, and stamp,
As if both legs were tingling with the cramp.
At length they pack—and silence for a minute
Pervades 'the House' and all 'the Commons' in it.
Now then, or never, 'Mr. Speaker, state
The cause and question of this stern debate!'
'That Tweedle-dum (by National decree),
Lose his precedence over Tweedle-dee?'

Anser rose first;—Gloom from his presence fell
O'er all—and well-nigh rose the House as well,
Mov'd as by (ringing of a dinner bell);
Anser, whose hardy youth (majestic work)
Supplied our Indian armaments with pork;—
Whose ripen'd mind to injur'd Greece gave tone,
And almost made her honest, by a loan;
Progressing time his heavy forehead decks
With laurels (transient growth of Middlesex);
Now older grown he fights by *Irus*' side,
An Irish Borough Town's imported pride.
'Sir,—I conceive the question not to be
The simple difference twixt a 'dum' and 'dee;'
'Tis an attempt of the 'illiberal swarm'
To check 'Retrenchment,' nullify 'Reform!'

Joseph Hume. Daniel O'Connell.

Sir,—I've a calculation showing clearly,
What the Reform Bill costs the Country yearly!
'Ten thousand pounds' to Barristers revising:
To Lawyers 'fifty thousand' for advising;
And 'fifteen thousand' more throughout the Nation
In 'splendid shillings'—price of 'registration;'
Value of time consum'd in showing grounds
For claims (none doubted), 'seventy thousand pounds.'
Another 'seventy' in vexatious tricks
And false objections—fair in politics;
And just 'one million,' at an easy guess,
For public Business blunder'd more or less!
Where is the product of this barren root?
'Tis fruit we ask, Sir! and we will have fruit!
The 'Tories' (seventy years this Nation's curse)
Drew not so largely on the public purse!
The thinking 'People' won't be put off thus,
And judge 'the Whigs' by measures—not by fuss.
Still, must 'paid Sinecures' at Court exist?
Must there be 'Poor Laws' and a 'Pension List?'
Must there be 'Borough-mongers' still? and must
Unbless'd evasions bow 'Reform' to dust?
We too who thought ourselves for life secure,
Are clearly getting every Session fewer;
And though we battled for 'the cause of right,'
And free'd the Nation in her own despite,
Yet—this 'Third Parliament' beholds the foes
Of Economical Reform in rows
Equivalent to ours:—a sight which gladdens
The Squires, and the productive classes maddens!

Sir,—At a future period I shall move
For papers and returns this fact to prove.
Meanwhile, th' amendment which I would be at—
Runs thus—'To leave out all words after 'that,'
In order, Sir, to substituting these :—
'Henceforth—be neither 'Tweedledums' nor 'dees!''
He said ;—and sat him down in doleful dump :
Then *Typho* started up with panic jump.
So have I seen in some neglected street
Heroic Punch his startled audience greet.
Him Ireland sent inveterate, to bore
Our English patience with one Curran more.
Long time in flowery metaphors he show'd
His Country's wrongs and groan'd beneath the load;
Till, lull'd to rest by Greenwich and white-bait,
He left those wrongs to Normanby and Fate.
'Say, Mr. Speaker! can such laws be just?
You, Sir, must know—I say again, you must—
That Ireland, jewel of the Western seas
(Land of potatoes, Moore, and absentees),
Land of my birth—by faction tempest-toss'd,
Bemoans in 'Orange' weeds her interests cross'd.
Pass me this bill!—a little boon;—you won't?
We need it!—granted. Pass it!—No? then don't!
Wait till indignant millions quit their lair,
And strong in moral grandeur back the prayer!
I see ye cowering, crouching, quivering, quaking,
I see the Orangemen and Tories shaking!
Ireland asserts, amidst a World's applause,
Equality in railroads, rights, and laws;

Richard Lalor Shiel.

I charge you—all who hold your Country dear!
All who can spare to slavery a tear!
All who can groan with Poland, burn with Gaul!
Firebrands of Liberty, I charge ye all!
Aid not, abet not, bear not tyranny!
Why should this 'dum' precede this modest 'dee?'
This lordly 'Tweedledum!'—But hist!—those sneers,
Those groans!—I scorn them while a Nation cheers!
I see a day, a brighter day in store!
Pardon me, Liberty! I see a score
Radiant with moral sunshine!—Ireland casts
The slough of ages to the envious blasts;
And panoplied in youthful vigour says:—
'I'd like to see the man who daur say 'Pays!''
He said—and next day said the general Town,
'Great as his rising was his sitting down!'
This peroration was so monstrous fine,
Most men retir'd to think it o'er, and dine.

As the fierce storm that burst, in torrents forth,
And all the rigour of the blust'ring North,
Lulls to a calm, and drops in mizzling rain,
To rave in fiercer gusts, and waste the plain;—
The shepherd and his flock for shelter race:—
So—in debating tempests, there's a space
Sacred to 'Dulness' and young 'Modesty;'
Heavy-stern'd fowls, and chicks that learn to fly;
But most to Dulness;—now in Court she sits,
And makes her oldest favourites pass for wits.
Complaisant hears th' excruciating work
They make with writhing 'Pitt,' and tortur'd 'Burke,'

While pointless 'Chatham' babbles it away,
And 'Fox' talks nonsense more than once a-day.
This space its rightful owners handled well,
But what they said it profits not to tell.
Enough that weightiest matters were discuss'd,
And facts that fail'd in proof were ta'en on trust;
With all the grave parade of pompous rules,
That makes a 'prig' the very prince of fools.

To empty benches this at least belongs,
If they lack ears they hold no mocking tongues.
Few sounds impede the legislator's throes,
Save where reporters blow th' impatient nose.
The Speaker dozes in his awful chair,
And ills he may not fly from strives to bear.
The Serjeant agitates himself and sword;
The 'triple clerkdom' looks supremely bor'd;
The Strangers yawn with energy, and cough,
In tones that mean at least, the 'Pit's' off! off!
Yet still these pond'rous Statesmen blunder on!—
Thank Heaven, the House has fill'd, and their reign's done!

Then *Irus* rose and grimly sneer'd around,
And clutch'd in act to speak his wig profound.
'Irus,' Milesian 'Irus!' burlier rogue
Than Cleon or Jack Cade when most in vogue.
To different champions special gifts belong;
Some are adroit, some cunning, and some strong.
Some grasp the pike; these hurl the quiv'ring dart,
Those draw the sword!—To scatter dirt his art.

Daniel O'Connell.

This talent rais'd him,—and this art maintains:
Thus pockets he the 'Bondsmen's' wretched gains.

'Sir! I predict this measure too will feel
The teeth of those who snap at Ireland's weal.
Yes!—there in snarling enmity ye sit;
Monopolists of all but truth and wit.
I bid ye pass this bill! Yes, Beasts! I bid ye!
Ye thought to catch me tripping—marry, did ye?
'Tories' and 'Orangemen,' I hold the brief!
Virtue demands and Ireland claims relief!
Ireland my friend, my client, and my fee!
Dear are a thousand pounds of thine to me!
Dear are thy Boroughs! and thrice dear thy Peasantry,
Who burn in jest, and knock at head in pleasantry.
Dear is my great position, given by fate,
Cloy'd with dull homage from the men I hate.
But ask for Justice here!—oh, save her name
From foul connexion with such public shame!
Ask charity of misers! sense of him
Who scatters thousands on a woman's whim:
Ask Whigs for place, My Lady for a l—se!
But oh! for justice never ask this House!'
Cries of 'Oh! oh!'
'Take back those yells again!
There needs no shout to make your rancour plain!
The Whigs are pledg'd to radical Reform!
The Ministry must dread a Tory storm!
For who but zealous Ireland steps between
Their hardy rivals and the British Queen?

This healthful measure then must pass—nay more,
If it don't pass, I die upon your floor.'
'Eight millions,' strong in peaceful agitation
And holy temperance, shall control the Nation;
And rabid brutes, sworn foes to Ireland's weal,
Who'd drug a cup, or hire a bravo's steel,
A vile, bloodthirsty, mercenary crew,'——
Cries of 'Oh! oh! chair! chair!' and 'Doodle-doo!'
'Hold, beastly bellowers!' 'Oh! oh! chair! chair!'
The Speaker rises with impressive air;
'Irus' meanwhile retorts with vulgar stare,—
'The Honourable Member must retract
'Th' expression, 'Beastly bellowers;' that's a fact!'
Well, then ('tis sweet apologies like this
Can heal the Commons' honour when amiss).
'Well, if compell'd, I do! but are they not so?
In any other place they would be thought so!
Then why not here?' With that there rose again
The savage hum of irritated men;
Because the House yawns, grumbles, groans, or shrieks,
Proportionate as rogue or ruffian speaks.
Sneers on his lip, and hatred in his frown,
The baffled Irus mutter'd and sat down.

Instant to him in withering scorn replied
Great *Diomedes*—and in terms defied.
Clear in his reas'ning, classic in his style,
In action various, just, and versatile;
Without a rival in the lists of wit,
His fancy charm'd where most his satire bit.

Lord Stanley.

For gentle blood best gives that graceful ease,
For lack of which our clowns so seldom please.
None knew the 'Beggarman's' requirements better,
And none was less inclin'd to be his debtor.
'Sir,—I rejoice to see this House thinks fit
That no impediments should hamper wit!
The scene just over seems a little coarse,
But who would gain in polish and lose force?
Did I, like some, admire the learned Irus,
I'd whisper in his ear, that rules require us
To sink vile language and scurrility,
And bid a gentleman use courtesy.
But, since it is observ'd that men impeach
Authorities remov'd above their reach;
I waive the subject,—and at once proceed
To the 'great cause' in which he's yearly fee'd.
When fierce impatience of our country's pains
Fires noble souls to break unworthy chains,
With their high names the meanest cottage rings,
And patriots rank before the wisest kings.
But, when cupidity and falsehood join
To cheat a people, and to filch their coin;
When the High Priest of Freedom's sacred fire
Plays 'Cato's' part for despicable hire;
Opinion stamps and circulates his shame,
And fools who trusted execrate his name.
Too plastic Ireland! in designing hands
Shall Priestcraft arm and rogues direct thy bands?
Shall vile harangues breed crime in every shape,
And 'dupes' be hang'd that 'demagogues' may 'scape?

Is it thy joyous peasant's natural turn
To rob and slay, assassinate and burn?
No!—fiendish prompters do the bus'ness better,
And murder safely in a speech or letter.
Oh, much-deluded Country! why so keen
For 'Home-bred Parliaments' on College Green?
I too in sober earnest will appeal
To Erin's wrongs,—and cauterise to heal!
From me, at least, the subtle Irish Kerne
His 'leader's' selfish arts shall plainly learn!
Shall see himself in true but paltry light,
The 'vane of priestcraft,' and the 'tool' of spite;
His starving babes with empty speeches fed—
(Sackcloth for covering, and stones for bread).
The desperate feuds of Cromwell's hated sway,
Fresh as the 'Ribbon outrage' of to-day,
The war of rival races unanneal'd—
The Country now, as ever, discord's field.
Shake off the Demagogues whose iron hold
Strangles thy rising trade to clutch thy gold!
Give every 'Freeman' liberty to vote,
Whatever button's on his Sunday coat;
Distrust thy Patriots that with double face
Sell thee for power—an office—or a place!
Retrench in 'agitation!' dare to be
What these will never make thee—really free!'

This great debate now totters to its close!
The clock struck 'Twelve'—and wise *Ulysses* rose.

The Right Hon. Sir Robert Peel.

A man he was by long experience sage,
And the completest Statesman of his age!
Much had he suffer'd!—labour'd much—and seen
Good times and bad, and middling intervene,
And weather'd all of them,—design'd to float
On roughest seas the best—like 'Deal Life-boat!'
He was too shrewd to patronise the flash
Of generous ardour which the world calls 'dash.'
His wisdom was the theme of praise with many;
His caution was scarce popular with any.

'Sir, never leader of an Opposition
Was placed before in such a droll position.
To save the noble Ajax from his friends,
On my good nature once again depends.
Am I to patch each crude disjointed bill,
And tell him what his own enactments mean?
Up to this moment there are just fourteen
Important measures—that there's not a doubt of—
I've help'd him into, pull'd him through, or out of.
Let him look to it, from this hour I strike;
Then let his friends run riot as they like!
The present measure, Sir, appears to be
Childish in terms, and false in policy.
To agitate for ever, and invent
Food for dispute in things indifferent,
Is full as dang'rous to the Commonwealth
As ceaseless action to the body's health.
Did not the noble Ajax plainly state
His fix'd opinion on this point of late?
These were his words at Edinburgh—'We
Must keep the 'Bill' in its integrity!

Guard its provisions, cling to, and defend it
From all who'd mar it, and from all who'd mend it;
And give the great experiment full scope
To work responsive to a Nation's hope!'
While yet Reform depended, I was one
Who taxed its schedules in no measur'd tone;
But what the wisdom of the land thinks fit,
Finds me submissive to superior wit;
I bow to laws I labour'd to reject,
And sink my private judgment in respect.
Then, for Reform, from its own Sire I claim
Respect as mark'd, and deference the same.
Let him not, quiv'ring like the aspen-tree,
Shake with the breath of every policy;
Nor chop and change regardless of disgrace,
For that poor gaud, another year of place!'

Then *Ajax* much beset by friends and foes,
But guiltless of one thought of yielding, rose.
Simple and clear his undiscursive mind,
And unadorn'd his views, but not confin'd;
With ne'er a brilliant quality he'll act,
In nice conjunctures, with the keenest tact.
None cares so little when he's in a mess.
Reproach don't stir him, nor can jibes distress!
But now he flounder'd in the foulest plight
That e'er befell administrative wight.
Here Irus, his protecting Genius, skinn'd him;
There his own words and wise Ulysses pinn'd him.

Lord John Russell.

'Sir, I may be allow'd to deprecate
The inconvenient heats of this debate.
I think it most unwise, for no good reason,
To press this "question" at the present season;
When Government has been of late preparing
A general measure it may fairly share in.
And since 'tis so, the learned 'Irus' surely
Claims my support a little prematurely;
His zeal outruns his judgment—on reflection,
Perhaps he'll see the facts in this connexion.
The wise 'Ulysses,' too, may rest assur'd
The points he thinks in danger are secur'd.
The words he quoted from a speech of mine
At Edinburgh, were not spoke with that design,
Nor did I utter them in that relation,
And must impeach their present application.
When I declar'd the Bill a 'final measure,'
Of course, I meant 'twas final during pleasure
Of Parliament: indeed, what Legislation
Can force prospective measures on the Nation?
My meaning then was this, that things arrang'd
By law remain in force until they're chang'd.
Is it for me to compromise my friends?
Define where National improvement ends;
Or cramp my better judgment by design?
These may be Tory arts—thank Heaven, not mine!
Of all administrations that is worst
Where colleagues' free opinions are coerc'd!
This is an 'open question!' can I get
Together a consentient Cabinet?

Could wise 'Ulysses' on a late occasion,
With all his happy talent at persuasion?
Sir, I can sacrifice rank, power, and place,
But am not yet prepar'd to brook disgrace;
Can fling the bauble 'Office' to the wind;
But cannot force one conscientious mind.
An interchange of confidence endears
Colleagues,—unites them,'—(ministerial cheers);
'Strengthen's them'—(cheers); 'identifies their cause
With purest liberty.'—(immense applause.)

MARGEITES—'THE FLOUTER.'

It is said that Homer wrote a book under this signature.

The Praises of Tobacco.

1840.

Oh mild and civilising 'real Havannah!'
How shall I laud thee in a fitting manner?
Before thy mystic influence fade away
The cares and sorrows of man's little day,
Thou canst 'knit up the ravell'd sleeve of care,'
And to a courtier turn the rustic bear;
And Cymon would have ta'en a polish one rub higher,
Had he but smok'd to fair Iphigeneïa.

Thee doth the Dutchman honour in his swamp,
Potent ally of 'schnaps,' and foe to damp!
Thee the 'vieille moustache' of a hundred fights,
Who strikes for glory, and the People's rights!
Thee doth the 'Tiger' lounging in the Park,
And thee the cockney 'prentice on a lark;
And thee Spain's black-ey'd daughters—bless 'em for it!
Most of our Ladies from their souls abhor it,
And vow that they will always say him nay
Who of his throat shall dare to make a chimney.
Thee doth the jolly tar of Nelson's school,
Born when Britannia o'er the waves had rule.
See him laid up, in age mature and ripe,
At 'Greenwich,' quaff his ale and smoke his pipe!

Nor does he dream that 'tis against the laws
Of public order—even when he 'chaws!'
Thee did the parson of the good old sort,
Sweetest ally, and mutual friend of Port;
Thee doth the sportsman by the covert-side,
The solace of a wintry two-hours' ride;
Thee doth the jolly landlord!—so do I!
Now do you really wish me, by-the-bye,
To give it up? 'You do?'—Then I won't try,
For nought more sovereign doth the Leech possess,
To cure those ills which on frail nature press.
And if you're ever stretch'd on Love's fierce rack—oh!
You'll not be cured by rhubarb, but tobacco!

Fables though deem'd by many—there are tales
Of ancient mariners in wondrous gales,
Who worn by days of watching, nights of fear,
Far from their reck'ning borne, they knew not where,
Have seen,—o'er coral reefs, through rainless skies,
Dim forms of shadowy islands fitful rise.
These have they deem'd abodes of perfect rest;
Fortunate islands,—islands of the blest!
And told in after years—when round the fire,
As howls the blast, men draw their chairs the nigher;
'How the mild land-breeze on its bosom bore
Sabæan odours from the teeming shore;
And goodly shapes were seen, and Siren lays
(Sweet as the dreams of childhood's happy days),
Came, lightly wafted,—as the dimpled sea
Rippled in measure to their melody.'

Could they have near'd the Lotus-eater's shore?
The dreamy land Ulysses trod before;
Or were those cliffs, for so't might be, the while,—
But wand'ring bulwarks of '*St. Brandon's isle?*'

'Twas none of these! those lands, that happy ground,
None but an ancient mariner e'er found;
Nurtur'd a little in Munchausen's school,
And fond of spinning yarns,—but still no fool!
Yet born, ere homewards, so had Fate decreed,
Sir Walter Raleigh brought the Indian weed;
And, though we bless him hourly when it rains,
Got nothing but a ducking for his pains.

These were the lands where, smiling now, expand
Havannah's plains and Cuba's palm-clad strand!
Ere yet the mighty mind reflecting found,
By potent reasons, that the world was round;
And Colon, lucky turn in Fortune's wheel,
Gave a new world to Leon and Castile;
Long ere the vast Atlantic's bosom bore
Pizarro's legions to the groaning shore,
And Spanish blood-hounds quaff'd Peruvian gore.
Ere in the fair new World the villain, Gold,
Gave life to crimes unheard of in the old;
And ruffian days sent forth the Buccaneer,
Kite of the Ocean, on his fell career;
And Jesuit Fathers spread, with bloody hand,
Christ's mild religion o'er the fainting land.

'St. Brandon's Isle.' Atlantis.

Here, bless'd with wealth he toil'd not to increase,
The simple native smok'd the 'pipe of peace.'
Arcadian bliss!—serene repose of soul!
From untax'd pouch he fill'd his ample bowl,
Or listless wand'ring in the sunny glade,
With dex'trous twist the light cigar he made.
Nature so largely flung the fragrant weed
O'er hill and dale—this, this was bliss indeed!

The Old Story.

1839 or 1840.

LOVE in some souls is fleeting! Be it so!
I would not change their laughter for my woe!
Yes! dream of rapture in mine early youth,
I, like to other fools, believed thee 'sooth:'
Gave loose to roving fancies, feared no ill,
And though convinced, would gladly dream on still:
For one fair image, cherish'd yet with tears,
Smiles through the vista of retiring years:
Mellowed perhaps in tint, but pure and light,
Like Claude's fair evenings delicately bright,
Here does it linger still, and will not part
Till death erase it from a broken heart!
Again, in mournful mood, and yet again,
I stir the ashes of this ancient pain,
And bend me o'er the censer's drooping flame,
Whence all my joy and all my sorrow came.

There are who hold that Time can mellow grief:
Maybe some find it so—but what relief
Is treasured for that soul whose every start
Wrenches the barb that rankles at the heart?
Would that some early storm had stranded me
On a lone island of the pathless sea,

Ere waking dreams had cruelly defined
The vacant longings of an ardent mind;
With Crusoe's solitary sceptre blessed,
There had I found, perhaps, unvalued rest!
Or, shunned in cares enforc'd, and savage toil,
Gains heartless round and giddy life's turmoil,
An Eremite indeed, forbid to rove
In error through the paths of hopeless Love.

A flower more lovely than the new-blown rose
In some sea-beaten island haply grows.
Doubtless a maid more lovely there might be!
Yet was she all that Love could dream to me,
And 'twixt our hearts perhaps was sympathy.
Ay! there's the rub! when kindred souls combine
In sweet accordance pedants can't define,
Then infant Love to tropic growth expands,
And knits two beings by the gentlest bands;
Yet strong as cradled Hercules it shakes
The loosened coils of Envy's strangled snakes.
Ideal beauty's form we view displayed
And link its attributes to one dear maid;
Child of our fervid fancy starts to-day,
Perfection clad in unideal clay.
This is the dream! These are the pangs I felt!
This is the image at whose feet I knelt—
To grasp this shadow, fondly, wildly strove,
In all the fierce idolatry of Love!

How smooth is life to those, how flatly sweet
Who only live to earn the bread they eat!

Whose greatest cares from little nothings rise;
A rustic holiday their chiefest prize;
And this their fitting epitaph,—'Here lies
'A man not passing foolish, nor too wise:
'A stately man, of wit profound and dark,
'A pattern beadle or a parish clerk:
'His death was sanctioned by his widow's tears,
'His life a blank of threescore useless years!'

'Twere better thus to drawl away life's span;
In all the finer feelings less than man.
One of those 'ciphers'—well if 'twere no worse—
Which swell the total of the Universe.
Not all can figure in the chiefest place,
Nor give denomination to their race.
Few minds can carry out th' heroic tone
That claims all men's obedience, follows none!
From toil and danger most men shrink aside,
And recreant numbers single recreants hide,
For where so many falter who can chide?
Yes! it were better!—who would not be such
But that they know, and think, and feel too much?
O bless'd Simplicity of hand and heart,
To find thy substitute surpasses art!
Rated by others happy—rating them
The joyous hearts, and careless blades they seem,
How do we miss of truth? 'twere strange to tear
The veil from human follies, and lay bare
A conscience struggling with untold remorse
And guilt,—and all from doing 'things of course!'

Drown recollection! trifle as ye may:
Drink deep! laugh loudly! revel it to-day!
Still fearful thoughts unbidden intervene
Of what we are, and what we might have been;
For ranker springs on battle-fields the grain,
And boist'rous mirth oft dwells with secret pain.

Ah, Disappointment! ever-welling draught!
Still full, still brimming though so often quaffed!
Yes! Marah's bitter streams must yield to thee,
And the dead waters of that sullen sea
Where once a Patriarch's eyes desir'd in vain
The glorious cities of the Godless plain.
And still—so runs the Eastern Tale—appear
Once—at the close of every hundredth year—
Halls, terraced gardens, towers of antique mould,
And shapes disgraced in riot as of old.
These has the evening fisherman beheld,
A warning pageant of unhallowed eld,
Just as the ling'ring rays of passing light
Speckle the forehead of advancing night;
And light and darkness for the moment seem
Balanced, like joy and grief, in youthful dream.
The gloaming time—a neutral space on earth—
When visions roll together—ghosts have birth—
And fairy music rings from haunted dell—
And 'Genii' 'scape from 'Soliman's' dark spell—
The mighty 'name of God,' more strong than all;
Dungeon, or chain, or Hell's custodient wall.

So now farewell! my mind is fixed to roam
Where seas may bear me farthest off from home.
Where no brown nightingale my pains shall move;
Nor strike the chords, nor sing the notes of love.
Till desolate at heart, and crushed in strength,
The weary pilgrim hesitate at length,
Pluck the fat rushes for a dying bed,
And roll a log to prop his aching head,
While gathering vultures from afar descry
The sinking wretch, and scream to see him die.
Still in this last extremity, alone,
Unwept, unpitied, friendless, and unknown;
True to the last, to one fair image true,
Thy form, dear girl, shall hover in my view;
Such as I knew thee once—ere wretches strove
To wean thy young affections from first love,
And sent me forth—scorning, and scorn'd again—
To wander hopeless round the world, like Cain.

The Crisis.

PART I.

DECEMBER 12, 1846.

'Did they not next compel the Nation
To take and break the Protestation?
To swear and after to recant
The solemn League and Covenant?
To take th' Engagement and disclaim it,
Enforced by those who first did frame it?'
Hud. Part II. Canto II.

'SURPRISED,' I think you said;—my friend, how young
The man who can believe a Statesman's tongue!
A clamorous life of absolute negation
Adds pith and weight to tardy affirmation;
As restive witnesses compelled to admit
The point they fight against, establish it.

Five years ago Peel followed the stout plough;
Whistling as farmers scarce will whistle now.
Turning up power and place—a glorious crop!
'Twas hard to say precisely where he'd stop.
So bas'd upon the wishes of the Nation,
(Tired of Whig humbug) seem'd 'Sir Peel's' vocation;
But since he turned a turf with '*ten-pound spade*,'
And wheel'd it off, by Hudson's barrow's aid;

'*Ten-pound spade.*' This refers to the opening of one of Hudson's lines, when Her Majesty Queen Victoria was the guest of The Right Hon. Sir Robert Peel (Her Prime Minister), at Drayton, and the public were made aware that the first turf (which was cut by Sir Robert) was wheel'd away in a barrow that was a work of art, and that the spade he had us'd cost ten pounds.

Since Bright has seen new lights, while Cobden spoke ;
(I wonder, in hot weather, these don't choke ;)
Since 'Great Macaulay' has discoursed the Scotch,
And given them their own dainty, a hotch-potch ;
And Edinborough's Provost has declar'd
He would not be by London out-Lord-Mayor'd
In matters appertaining to the League,—
Cant, balderdash, bad English, and intrigue.
Since these portents, like baleful comets, have
Appalled the timid, and abash'd the brave ;
Ending in sudden *ex-ephippiation*
Of the late rider who bestrode the Nation ;
It may be forbidden us to eye him
In solemn sadness—since we lose much by him.

Gifted with tireless energy, fair speech,
Prudence, and never-equalled mental reach,
Like 'Will-o'-th'-Wisp,' thou'st led thy sheep astray,
And left them flound'ring in the miry way :
The silly flock, whose wool has kept thee warm
In many a searching wind, and biting storm.
'Twas a vile freak !—but how were we to check it,
Although thou wast out-Thomasing A'Beckett ?
And as that Bishop, when he once had got
The boiling (safe) of Cantuarian pot ;—
So, hast thou proved intractable as mule ;
When snugly seated in the chair curule.

'*Ex-ephippiation.*' I have no excuse to offer for the coining of this word, excepting that I think that no other word that I know of, or could make, expresses my meaning so well.

And now, thou servest those who placed thee there,
Worse in thy fall than Hudibras the bear;
Who ne'er had ta'en such harm from foes in fight,
As from descending squelch of friendly knight.

The farmer now, his friends and party gone,
Shall be a meal for Cobden or Lord John;
Betray'd by those in whom he plac'd most trust,
His Coalition levell'd with the dust;
Thou wilt not e'en conduct his funeral,—
Nor lend a decent hand to smooth his pall;
Brought to death's door by thy new '*sliding rigs*,'
Thou leav'st him to be buried by the Whigs.

Gramercie for such advocates! but when
Will prudence teach, or history warn men?
The fault was theirs, who needs must trust once more
The man who'd failed them at their need, before.

Are not thy followers dragg'd here and there,
Like mastiffs clinging to a baited bear?
To their astonishment,—for who can spy
Through all the mazes of thy policy?

'*Sliding rigs.*' Sir Robert Peel, whether with an eye to the future, or to the requirements of the age, invented and brought in what he call'd a 'sliding scale.' The transition from this state of things, to no scale at all, was not unnatural; and yet the treason was so patent, that it had a greater effect upon public confidence, and impair'd the value of public morality to a greater extent, than any other measure that I recollect within the range of an experience of forty years.

Now Maynooth calls,—and now O'Connell thunders
Justice,—Repeal,—and other Irish wonders.
Now—Corn-law-drummer Cobden sounds to arms,
With well-devis'd and popular alarms;
Roaring Free-Trade,—cheap bread,—and famine cries!—
And—praising Manufacturers to the skies.

To each and all thou yieldest more or less;
And they get most, who most unseemly press:
For which they thank thee not!—but reckon it
A tribute to their power, or their wit.

We can look on unmov'd, while Smith O'Brien
Plays (by desire) the part of 'Irish Lion:'
While burly Daniel patters fierce complaints,
And foams out eulogies on 'Yankee Saints,'
Whose money's to be '*rinted*,'—and then sputters
Something about 'Commissioners,' and 'gutters;'
But when a party, banded to prevent
Continual change, and wild experiment,
Entrusted to Peel's guidance, and so long
In all the energy of union strong;

'*Rinted.*' 'Daniel O'Connell' made a good stock in trade, about this time, of some American brothers, who contributed on paper to his rent. We used to think that he did not always realise the amount of the subscriptions publish'd; but upon the whole, it is my opinion now, that he got a fair per-centage on them. He was an able-bodied agitator, and a sharp lawyer; and did more (in fact) to advance the cause of Ireland (whatever that may be) than all the 'Currans,' 'Grattans,' 'Floyds,' 'Fitzgeralds,' 'Napper Tandies,' 'Shearses,' and the rest of the long line of pleasant fellows that have taken up the business because it bound them to nothing.

Falls, on the sudden, with no power to save,
Into a yawning suicidal grave ;
We search for cause sufficient for the crash !
And bring *him* in—sole author of the smash.

Retire to Tamworth ! History possesses
True portraits of thee, in thy several dresses.
The light fantastic costume of thy youth,
When thou didst shape 'gold currency' forsooth ;
The good old coat in which thou didst discharge
Thine hest to Oxford ;—sober, decent, large.
The battered 'redingote' that wrapp'd thee round,
What time (being weigh'd) thou first wast wanting found.
But how to limn, or anyhow convey
A notion of thy 'Joseph's coat' this day,
Will far exceed the *fresco feats* of all
Whose hands shall dabble on Saint Stephen's wall.

MARGEITES.

'*Fresco feats.*' About this time there was a talk of conveying the results of the genius of the age to posterity, under the masque of fresco. Certain pots of scalding materials were prepar'd, and much musty learning and research call'd into play. Everybody took it for granted that the old-fashion'd plan of painting on canvas, without trick and quackery, was as much to be avoided as a man who yawned during the great plague of London. We should be fortunate now if some of the fine pictures painted at that time had been executed in the condemn'd fashion. In their present condition they resemble nothing so much as one of Mr. Whistler's 'arrangements.'

The Crisis.

PART II.

DECEMBER 21, 1846.

'The solemn League and Covenant
Shall seem a mere God d—n me rant.'
Hud. I. Canto.

HAIL, furious Cobden! Corn-law errant knight!
Prepar'd alike to argue, jest, or fight.
Force on the goodly scheme so long since plann'd,
Foreclose the mortgages, and take the land!
Strike while the iron's hot, and farmers reel
Under the blows administer'd by Peel.
Laugh down all those whose rustic speech betrays
An inclination to old English ways.
All squires are jolterheads, all lords are fools,
And he rules England best whom clamour rules.

Who clothed the Universe in cotton print?
Who first coined fortune in the railway mint?
Who first made needles, pins, and patent blacking?
Who first sent 'vile monopoly' a-packing?
Who made cheap crockery? The farmer? No!
Enlightened Villiers, Cobden, Bright and Co.
Who can preserve the country through the millers?
Enlightened Cobden, Bright and Co., and Villiers!

Who scorn to deal in fiction and intrigue?
Who first turned tea-parties t' account?—The League.
There, nodding o'er bohea, our patriots sit,
Sweetening the draught with Anti-Corn-Law wit,
And chastened pleasantry, and through the fumes
The wise amongst them predicate the dooms
Of landlords, rents, tithes, taxes, and determine
The downfall of all drones, and such-like vermin.

Ye wide-mouthed doctors of a falling state,
As shrewd of wit, as courteous in debate,
As kind of heart, as tender of offence,
As full of wise device as common sense!
'Tis quite a luxury for us to view
Our old-world maladies shown up by you
In Covent Garden Theatre, and feel
That your sublime discussions influence Peel.
True liberality consists in sparing
A man's own purse and charitably sharing
The property o' th' unproductive classes
(Landlords and tenants) fairly 'mongst the masses.
Who sees not this is dang'rous and a fool,
And should be treated as a Tory mule.

Repeal the Corn Laws, and what dunce but knows
That you increase the sale of cotton hose?
Let corn be thirty shillings once, per quarter,
And every Englishman will drink his porter.
Trade must push out instanter, left and right,
As aloes grow five fathoms in a night;
And Manchester shall undersell all States,
In linsey-woolsey, cotton, and white plates.

A cunning fellow once assured a goose
He knew the way to make her wings produce
A double crop of quills. The bird, delighted,
Swore such a service ne'er could be requited,
And placed herself forthwith in hands of quack,
Who straight pulled every feather from her back.
'Now then,' said he, 'they'll grow again next year;
And thus you'll have a double crop, 'tis clear.'
Cobden's the quack of promises profuse!
And take care, farmer, that you're not the goose!

'Tis thought that Merlin prophesied these times,
And shadowed forth their splendours in these rhymes:
'From nineteen hundred years take fifty-three,
And then in 'merrie England' there shall be
For every spinning-jenny two or three!
And weavers, being better fed and stronger,
Shall work, at half the wages, two hours longer.
The farmers shall grow rich by Peel's devices
For raising taxes and for lowering prices.
And yet the dolts shall be the last to bless
His salves for agricultural distress.
In 'forty-five' a little man shall try
To make a much-enduring ministry:
But for his chance I won't give fivepence sterling,
Or any Whig's amongst 'em.—Thus saith Merlin!'

Ye corn-law saints, who with uplifted eye
The devil and the tax on bread defy,
Who revel in a grievance to reform,
Like Lapland witches, when they've raised a storm;

And thou, great Cobden ! whose select discourse
Invests old arguments with novel force,
Hold hard your corn-law besom for a space,
And meet a farmer fairly—face to face.

Is all this stir a blessing to the poor?
Are all this 'holy League's' intentions pure?
Swear by the God of harvests that you think
That wages, with the price of corn, won't sink !
Ye cannot ! dare not ! then forbear to claim
The change ye screech for in the people's name !
Ask in the name of 'millionaires,' prepared
To buy up land whenever land is shared !
'Tis as you said, last week, a war of classes;
Where 'Leaguers' treat us farmer-folk as asses.
The stalworth arm (once staple of the land)
Henceforth must truckle to the cunning hand.
Commerce (the pith and marrow of the State)
Divorces Husbandry, her lowly mate.
But take care, Cobden ! Husbandry's rough clan
In self-defence might gather to a man;
And peers of nature, and the House of Peers,
Might haply fall together by the ears;
To disadvantage of the natural wise,
Both in the struggle and the people's eyes.

MARGEITES.

The Crisis.

PART III.

DECEMBER 26, 1846.

So Whig devotion must not intervene
To free the Nation and to serve the Queen!
And 'Russell,' with ambition's prize nigh clutched,
Is fain to leave his mutton-broth untouched,
Like traveller swallowing one boiling sup,
That hears the railway bell and shout,—'Time's up!'

Ah, doubly born for England's woe was he
Who taught thy boyish hand calligraphy!
Say one thing this day, and the next disdain it!
But '*litera*,' *Lord John*, '*scripta*,' *Russell*, '*manet!*'
Swear you were misreported—and by dint
Of wrangling prove it! But ''fore George,' don't print!
A sage may twist his arguments at will,
But can't gainsay the witness of a quill
Plucked from the most unwise of Noah's birds,
To render permanent man's fleeting words.

Oft have I seen thee, 'Russell,' cross thy steel
In gallant conflict with that 'maître d'armes,' Peel;

'*Litera scripta manet.*' Lord John Russell's letter to the Bishop of Durham.

And said,—Well done, thou little one ! but still
Power is indifferently supplied by will.
Thou art not 'cunning at the fence' like him,
Nor half so strong of wrist, nor large of limb.
And this time—(but 'tis neither 'round,' nor 'bout,'
Where Peel comes in again before he's out !)
This time, thy star, opinion, and thy foes,
Have bobbed th' official cherry 'neath thy nose,
And when thou opened'st thy mouth to swallow
Have shouted,—'Hark back, Russell ! hark back ! halloo !'
The clown won't mystify old Pantaloon
The whole of Christmas to a scurvier tune.

But here the Muse 'in doleful dump' must paint
The consternation of each suffering saint,
Prepar'd to share with thee the thankless toil
Of holding 'place,' and facing this turmoil.
Those who came up in 'special trains' returned
As 'third-class passengers,' with fares not earned.
And all the mob of Peel-defying rout
(Who talked rebellion when they thought him out),
Have such a dose to swallow at this time
As mocks description and makes bankrupt rhyme.
Go, muse on death i' th' Carlton's drawing-room,
Girt with blank faces and congenial gloom.
If that don't touch thee, I've no other plan
To make thee feel the littleness of man.

There, grouped in sullen knots, the rebels stand,
Averse to holding up the culprit hand ;

And strive in vain to catch a 'placeman's' eye,
As hint which words to stick to, which deny.
'Peel' babbles not,—and shrewd is he can say
What Peel has said,—or leastways what he may.
He blurts not out (like Russell) all he means,
But keeps his own good counsel, and the Queen's.
'Passive obedience' is his stone of touch,
And pliability's worth near as much :
We'll hope, in consequence, our Carlton friends
Have seen their error, and will make amends.

And how, prodigious whelps of Politics !
(English and Irish), like you these State tricks?
Lords of the movement here, and riot there,
Plain-spoken Cobden, Dan O'Connell hear !
Catch up Lord John ! Repeal's unwilling tool,
And send him, for a season, back to school !
His disposition to your cause is good !
He meant to serve it bravely—if he could.
But better his 'late speech' had died 'n abortion
Than smack'd so little of '*Auld Reekie's caution.*'
Besides, for private pique, or old dislike,
'Grey,' it would seem, declines to keep a pike
With 'Palmerston,' and failing him, 'tis clear
No Whig-born ministry could stand a year.

Come, Stanley ! buckle thy war-trappings on !
Disarm 'Sir Robert,' and defy 'Lord John !'

'*Auld Reekie's caution.*' Lord John's celebrated speech at Edinburgh. *Inde iræ.*

Young, noble, statesmanlike, mature thy plan!
The hour must soon be here—be thou the man!
The country can't as yet tell where to find
'Peel's' principles,—'Lord John's' ain't to its mind.
Cobden might make a railroad pay, or Bright
Manage a parish by his inward light;
Those 'Friar Bungays' of the State;—a class
Who promise England future walls of brass,
By battering down whatever ancient sages
Have thoughtfully built up in bygone ages.
But not a man amongst them can deceive
The moderate who pause, the wise who grieve.
When once the donkey brayed, his nasal din
Disarmed the terrors of the lion's skin.

MARGEITES.

The Traversers.

MARCH 25, 1844.

WHAT means this farce? this fever of the State?
This fortnight's trial and ten days' debate?
This galaxy of martyrs in the dumps,
These threaten'd jars, and jealousies, and thumps?
Say, gentle Muse! astonish'd 'Clio,' say!
What mean these patriots clad in prison grey?
These errant knights of liberty knock'd down
By one fell prosecution of the Crown?
Despite the peaceful strength of agitation,
And all the *weekly ballads of 'the Nation.'*
But how is this? What mean these downcast looks?
The tongue that falters, and the knee that crooks?
These puling tones of Traversers, that tell
Of 'Pennefather's' charge and Smith's cartel?
Where's the Rebellion so much talk'd of? Where
Are all O'Connell's castles in the air?
Where are the 'Scævolas' prepar'd to fry
Their dexter hands for Irish liberty?
Where is 'the Rent?' (fast falling off,—in spite
Of those who promise 'Pat' his soul's delight,
A mighty pretty difference and fight.)
Though 'Shiel' may bluster, Whiteside blaze, and all
The roaring crew of modern Currans bawl;

Though Corn-Exchange philippics shake the skies,
And Ireland swear she'll have 'Repeal,' or rise;
A *sober-minded Statesman* holds his course
Unmov'd by bluster, undeterr'd by force;
Sends beef and pork to victual Irish barracks,
And forwards regiments in 'barks and carracks.'
Then—prosecutes 'O'Connell' for a riot;—
Tries him forthwith;—convicts:—and all is quiet!

Oh, lame and impotent conclusion! Oh,
Parturient mountain, why deceive us so?
Is this the mouse that bred us such a pother?
The mouse that call'd 'America' god-mother?
Was it for this 'Repudiators' sent
Their weekly tribute to 'O'Connell's' rent?
Was it for this that 'Locofoco' rant,
And 'Yankee' jealousy, and liberal cant,
Fraterniz'd with 'Repeal,' and spat out gall,
And gloating prophesied 'Old England's' fall?
Biding the time when jackasses may try on
The tawny skin of England's fierce old lion.

Truly may Ireland's Agitator say,
''Tis mine to liberate and yours to pay.'

'*A sober-minded Statesman.*'—The Right Hon. Sir Robert Peel. A man (though it will be seen in the course of these 'Voices' that I separated from him upon a point which I could neither disguise nor look over) whom I once had the pleasure of considering not only the Leader of the Party to which my inclinations and judgment led me to belong, but, right or wrong, a giant.

Truly may Ireland answer—'Cease thy brag,
Judas ere this was trusted with the bag!
Restore the moneys thou hast had!—or show
That huge bombast can strike, at need, one blow!'
Ere many centuries have fleeted by,
Nay, years—perhaps ere yonder infant die—
This paper fabric of fictitious wealth,
This bloated insolence of too great health
Which men call commerce, shall collapse, and all
This shrine of Mammon totter to its fall,
The great anomaly resolved at last,
And England's glories scatter'd with the past.
Insurable no more—shall every breeze
Waft to her ports returning Argosies.
Driven from her stormy empire on the main,
England may drag, perhaps may hug a chain.
Her iron causeways crumbling into rust,
Her strength decayed, her mighty spirit crushed,
And Speculation (born with her) shall die,
And liberal arts and chastened Liberty.
This is the goal to which all States have come,
From classic Greece to iron-handed Rome.
And how and why? for enemies in vain
Have laid their grasp upon the lion's mane.
Internal heats and civil wars combined
To work the ruin demagogues designed;
And suicidal blows avenged the cause
Of conquered nations and dishonoured laws.
A brighter wreath than 'Alexander' wore,
Or 'Scipio' won, or 'Cæsar's' temples bore,

Be his ; whose calm philosophy shall bind
The 'Sister Nations' in one kindred mind !
Shall bid them cease their strife, and learn, though late,
That foes to both have revell'd in their hate.
And deep damnation be his meed who rends
Ireland from England for his own bad ends.

The man who fosters 'jealousies and fears,'
And sows a crop that must be reap'd in tears ;—
Civil heart-burnings, jealous heats, and strife,
With all the woes unhinging social life ;—
Though 'Cap of Liberty' may deck his brow,
And gaping crowds before his footstool bow,
Sleeps not in calm repose !—No more than he
Who finds unbless'd renown at 'Tyburn Tree !'
Let him in state at 'Covent Garden' dine,
And plaster filth on Judges o'er his wine !
Let him bid hard for martyrdom ! and dare
The Law to strike, and force it not to spare !
Indignant after 'Ages' *shall deny,*
To such a 'Catiline,' their sympathy ;

'*Shall deny, to such a Catiline, their sympathy.*' Writing in 1844, I ventur'd on this prophecy, and now, in 1878, I find it has been fulfill'd to the letter. 'O'Connell' and his extraordinary performances have pass'd away from that inscrutable seat of judgment the Irish Mind. Indeed, nothing is more remarkable (from a philosophical point of view) than the stolid oblivion into which the name and memory of the most powerful 'Agitator and Demagogue' of modern times fell immediately upon his decease.

It is true that his shrewd common sense prevented him from going the lengths of the 'Younger Ireland Party,' which led them into Smith O'Brien's rebellion and the catastrophe of the 'Cabbage Garden ;' but

And all the profit of his long career
Shall be the 'Rent' he swallow'd up when here!

---

it is certainly worthy of notice that the name of so great a man should have dropp'd entirely from the list of 'Irish Cries.' We have heard of the name of 'Flood,' and 'Grattan,' and even of that crack'd-brain'd 'tout' of the French Directory, 'Napper Tandy,' who led 'General Hôche' into difficulties at 'Bantry Bay.' Lord Edward Fitzgerald is still mention'd with affection, together with others that I need not allude to; but 'O'Connell!'—Well! somehow or other, no one refers to him. It was only the other day that they gave him a statue. The 'dapper dog and charming poet, Moore,' preceded him by several years in that emptiest but still most natural compliment paid by Fashion to departed worth or notoriety. How can this be accounted for? I fear we must propose a dilemma to the admirers of the great Agitator. Either he deserv'd to be 'dis-remember'd,' or the Irish Nation is the most fickle and ungrateful that a man can work for.

Prometheus Vinctus.

(ONE OF MR. WEBSTER'S REJECTED COMEDIES.)

1844.

Scene: A Garden in the Richmond Penitentiary.

PROMETHEUS *discover'd polishing a 'Repeal Button' with his coat-sleeve.*

DRAMATIS PERSONÆ.

PROMETHEUS . .	*A Traverser.*
VULCAN . . .	*Governor of the Richmond Penitentiary.*
FORCE / DURANCE-VILE } .	*His Turnkeys.*
OCEANUS . .	*Mayor of Cork.*
CHORUS . . .	*Oceanidæ—Fishwives.*
MESSENGERS . .	*One, two, three, and four.*

PROMETHEUS.

WELL!—here I'm fast,—if 'Wylde' can't get me out
And getting plaguey pale, and dreadful stout!
[*Contemplates himself in the Penitentiary mirror.*
Bother that 'Peel!'—I thought 'twas all my eye!
But since you're in, 'Prometheus,' don't say die!
[*Bangs himself on the chest.*
In History you'll make a perfect figure,—
As sure as 'Royal Sheba' was a nigger.

The 'Rint's' progressing too—and 'Joinville' may
Be bothering the 'Sassenach' any day.
He's a ra-al tar, that boy!—But now let's see
What 'Oireland' sends her martyr'd son—that's me!
[*Pulls a list out of his pocket and reads.*
A haunch of venison—nine Westphalia hams,—
And sixteen pots of marmalades and jams,—
Six pairs of worsted socks,—twelve ditto cotton,—
Six dozen mellow pears—the Divels!—rotten,—
Rotten they mane!—a mighty aysy chair!

Enter FIRST MESSENGER.

'Me Lard!' they've just elected ye 'Lard Mayor!'

SECOND MESSENGER.

'Me Lard!' a deputation from the Bake-
-Ers of Doblin—with a monstrous cake.

THIRD MESSENGER.

'Me Lard!' a deputation from the Liffey's
Fishermen, with salmons and good wishes.

FOURTH MESSENGER.

'Me Lard!' a couple of old women!

PROMETHEUS.

Hold!
Henceforth let elderlings be not so bold!
We like 'em young and plummy!

OLD WOMEN (*aside*).

Divel doubt ye!
But young and plummy ones can do without ye!
[*Exeunt Old Ladies in a huff.*

PROMETHEUS.

But who are these whose dulcet tones can dress
Harmonious thoughts in sounds of loveliness?

Enter CHORUS.

OCEANIDÆ, *or* FISHWIVES, *bringing in a Sturgeon.*

They sing.

Ocean's chiefest strong-box we,
Rifling with our net, the key,
Plunder'd have, and hasten now,
With the sea-weed on our brow,
Heralding a royal prize
To Prometheus' longing eyes.

From the greenest ocean deeps,
Where the rolling porpoise sleeps,
Where the sulky turbot grows,
Where the snoring walrus blows,
He had wander'd,—but we caught him,
And in triumph here have brought him.

Dublin haddocks are no food
For Prometheus great and good.
No 'Pol-doody' ever yet
Worthy was of Ireland's pet.

Sturgeon, sturgeon, suits his 'naythur,'
With a trifle of the 'craythur.'

PROMETHEUS.

I thank ye, ladies! Will ye take a drink?
[*Ladies drink.*
Be dad! I told ye ye were thirsty!—think
How beautiful is whisky on the sly,
When 'Timperance' and 'Mathew' are not by.
The more by token,—when I took 'the pledge'
I kissed no book,—but just 'me' thumb-nail's edge.
Ye've brought a most uncommon splendid baste!
[*Walks up to the Sturgeon and inspects it.*
Royal, they say,—the compliment's good taste.
And now I'll tell ye—if I hadn't spent
Within 'two hundred' of my next month's rent,
I'd make yer fortins, dears!
[*Kisses his hand to the Ladies, who retire.*
Bye! bye! Be off!
And tell your friends I'm ay-sier of me cough.

OCEANUS, MAYOR OF CORK, *arrives, making some wry faces.*

OCEANUS.

Och, tear and ages! What a jaunting-car
The Divels gave me! Faith, I'll not be far
From broken-back'd to-morrow! For a 'tizzy'
I'll never stick—but hire a wizzy-wizzy,
And rumble back again to Cork in state.

PROMETHEUS.

'Mornin',' Oceanus! Ye'll take a sate
After journey, and a drop of thim
Raal Irish sperets!

OCEANUS.

Will a duck, Sir, swim?

[*Drinks.*

The Parties are here suddenly interrupted by the return of the CHORUS, *who sing.*

They bid us cringe to Saxon yoke
 And bow to English laws,
They bid us speak, as cowards spoke
 Who betray'd the cause,—
The cause 'Fitzgerald' sigh'd for,
The cause that 'Emmett' died for,
That the lover left his bride for
 By a cold hearth-stone;
The sacred cause of 'ninety-eight,'
That arm'd the humble and the great,
And failing left us desolate.
 Och, hone! Och, hone!
But we'll not do 't! we'll not do 't!
 Though all the world combine;
Chains cannot bind the patriot mind,
 And, Ireland dear! 'tis thine.
On Tara's hill we'll muster still,
 In spite of all their bands;
And at 'Clontarf,' with the green scarf,
 And oak-staves in our hands.

Promethus shall lead us,
No longer in vain!
He free'd us, he free'd us!
We'll free him again!
Och, honey, won't we?

OCEANUS.

Will ye jist be aysy?
Ye're fit to drive the 'Liberathur' crazy.
Be off, ye Divels! or else stow your talk;
And let me 'rade' him an address from Cork!

Address.

'To the much persecuted, admir'd, illustrious,
Periwig-pated, and robustious,—
Friend, father, agitator, rent-collector,
The poor-man's guardian, banker, and protector,—
The Mayor and Corporation of Cork City
Greeting;—That you're a pris'ner more's the pity!

CHORUS (*interrupting*).

Hurroo! hurroo!
A fig for you,
Mayor of Cork! Mayor of Cork!
If you're grumpy,
Stupid, humpy,
Prithee walk! prithee walk!
For Cork is a broth of a city
As ever you'll see upon land;
And the Mayor for a bumpkin is witty,
And sits when he's too drunk to stand.

PROMETHEUS.

Ladies, behave yourselves! I'm quite asham'd
To hear these little imperfections nam'd.
The Mayor's a good Repealer, and is sent
To soothe my feelings and increase my rent.
Judge then—if patriotic wonder struck me dumb
To hear ye spake before he'd nam'd the sum.

CHORUS.

We bow to thy decision,
  Most beautiful, most strong!
And crave thine high permission
  To own that we are wrong.
For thou art he must make us free,
  Though Britain thunder, No!
And Erin's steed at fullest speed
  Rushing to battle,
In the spirit-stirring cause
Of religion, rights, and laws,
  Must stop when thou say'st 'Who-ah!'
Though shots round him rattle,
  And before him stands the foe!

Enter VULCAN *in a great hurry, follow'd by* FORCE *and* DURANCE-VILE, *his turnkeys.*

VULCAN.

Me Lard! you're out! The five Law Lords have told
The other Lords that Smith has miss'd his hold
Of ye this time!

PROMETHEUS.

Kind Vulcan, say you so?
Oceanus, your hand! me boy, d'ye know
I'm Lawyer enough yet for nine such fellows?

OCEANUS (*listening*).

Hark how the joyful population bellows!

PROMETHEUS.

Send for me car-r,—bid Smith O'Brien come!
Sound every trumpet, and beat every drum.

Exeunt omnes, except the CHORUS, *who sing.*

He is out! he is out!
Come pass the glass about,
And send for the Liberator's chair;
For let what will hap, hap!
In his Liberator's cap
And button, he must take the air!

Oh, Father 'Tom Maguire,'
Is it just as ye desire?
Umbrellas to the left in a row;
With the jaunting cars so grand,
In line, as if on stand,
And us singing,—Bloody end to the Saxon oh!

And is it to your mind,
With the breechless boys behind,
And the Mayor and Corporation in the front?

All hip-hip-hip, hoor-a-a-a-ing,
Like Balaam's ass a-braying,
　　And determin'd any sodger to confront?

Sure, isn't it a sight
To turn a black-eye white
　　To 'say' him winking round at the boys?
While Erin's harper's strumming
As the Liberator's coming,
　　And delighting 'Merrion's' echoes wid his noise.

Then hoorah for Denman's Law!
And three cheers for Campbell's jaw!
　　Wid our compliments to 'Lyndhurst' and 'Brougham.'
But let 'em keep away
On the Saxon side the say,
　　Or their friends will be better of their room:—
　　And have nothing but their pictures in their room.

Life's Almanac.

1837.

LIFE is May to young maids
    Dreaming of a lover;
Life is May to young men
    Wand'ring the world over!
Ev'ry cloud is tipp'd with light;
Ev'ry prospect glitters bright;—
Life is glorious in their sight!—
    Ah, well-a-day!

Life is June to fond hearts
    Just grown sympathetic!
Life is June to bachelors
    Not as yet splenetic!
Through the wild-wood as they stray,
Summer breezes round them play!
Ev'ry bird sings—'Holiday!'
    More, more's the pity!

Life's July to loving pairs
    Not as yet dissemblers;
Life's July to 'Candidates'
    Just elected 'Members.'

Nature wears a riper hue,—
Heaven expands in deeper blue;—
But the year's no longer new!
Woe worth the day!

August 'tis to Heiresses
Wedding Men of Fashion;
Caught by needy selfishness
In the guise of passion.
Ripening corn would seem to say,—
'Laugh and sing while yet ye may!
Yours is but a little day.—
Winter's blasts rattle!

September 'tis to Ministers
Dining at the Palace;
Calling England's just complaints,
'Disappointed malice.'
Autumn's grapes their locks entwine:
Corn is theirs, and mighty wine;
Oil to make their faces shine
Cheerily, cheerily.

October 'tis to good men,
Prov'd and temper'd duly;
Mariners who rode it out
Through life's storms unruly.
Mellower beams the sinking Sun;
Air is chill, and skies are dun;—
Fall the sere leaves—ev'ry one—
Noiselessly, noiselessly.

November 'tis to old churls
    Gloating o'er their treasures;
Wasting thee, by keeping thee,
    Golden King of Pleasures!
Heartless slaves of sordid gain,
Yours be ev'ry racking pain!
Plagues, and fears, and man's disdain,
    Fall on ye! fall on ye!

December 'tis to me now,
    Chilling, and dreary!
Winter to a warm heart
    Hopeless and weary.
Winter's sports no more for me
Wake to mirth the old roof-tree;
Yet the logs blaze cheerily,
    As once for me.

Life is blank to me—whom
    Love's dreams forsake;
Why did I sleep in bliss?
    Or why awake?
Banish hope, and banish fear,
None shall pain where none can cheer!
Close the melancholy year!
    Mournfully, mournfully.

The View from Pentelicus.

WRITTEN AT ATHENS, DECEMBER 1845.

THE Wind is whistling o'er 'Pentelicus,'
And northward sweep 'Bœotia's' rolling hills :
Rich is this view of scenes illustrious ;
And valleys channell'd by historic rills !
Below lies 'Marathon,'—and far away
'Eubœa's' outlines gird the purple-bosom'd bay !

On either side, framing that picture fair,
Crags of huge stature cut the sky's deep blue ;
Thither through quarries must thy foot repair
Whence greatest 'Phidias' his marbles drew ;
Leaving a monument to every land ;—
For thieves have marr'd in vain the wonders of his hand.

Methought I heard the voice of other times
(When 'Greece' was paragon of arts and arms),
Upbraid relentless Fate, lament her crimes,
And mourn the fatal dower of her charms,
By 'Roman,' 'Turk,' and 'Scottish spoiler' woo'd,
That ever, for her spoils, the weary maid pursued.

States fall, and Cities crumble in the dust!
But here thou see'st the strongholds of Fame!
What are the honours of the Great and Just?
A passing empty sigh—a bootless name!
Yet is their memory sweet as vernal shower
That all the air embalms, and doubly scents the flower.

And 'Alexander' calls to doughty deeds,
And 'Pericles' to graceful arts of Peace.
See, where 'Leonidas' in glory bleeds,
Leaving a never-dying flame in Greece:
For still among her hills they tell the tale,
How his unrivall'd day made 'Xerxes'' armies quail.

Now is the vow of many years fulfill'd,
And I (cold native of the merchant North),
That long have lov'd thee,—and e'en there could build
A shrine to lost Perfection and pass'd Worth—
At last approach thy presence;—but how chang'd
Thy glorious Rock!—how dumb the 'Groves' where 'Plato' rang'd!

Whistle then, chilling Wind!—thou chimest well
With Grecian fortunes present and to come!
Thou soundest on mine ear like passing bell:—
The fold's beset with wolves,—the dogs are dumb!
And the frail promise of a happier day
Is pass'd—for ever pass'd--in German gloom away!

Lacedaemon.

WRITTEN OFF THE COAST OF CAPE MATAPAN, 1845.

THOU hast perish'd, 'Lacedæmon,'
With thine iron-handed sons!
The 'Wall-less City' slumbers
Amid the fallen ones!

Through marshes and vile hovels
'Eurotas' takes his way;—
But thy name is fresh as ever,
And thy deeds shall last for aye!

Fierce thou wast, and valiant;
And valour show'd in thee,
Like a lion by a well-side,
Or a rock-bound coast at sea!

And the Nations from a distance gaz'd
In wonder, and in fear;
And shudder'd to awaken
The terrors of thy spear!

Gold could not tempt thy leaders,
  Nor death appal thy ranks!
Thou wast savage in thy penalties,
  And sparing of thy thanks!

And around thee grew a people
  Severe of speech and hand,
True to their friend—fierce to their foe,—
  Majestic, simple, grand.

There is 'Tœnarus!' and 'Malea!'
  And 'Taygetus' capp'd with snow!
But where is 'Lacedæmon,'
  That laid bright 'Athens' low?

Where are thy sturdy Nobles,
  Thine 'Ephors,' and thy Kings?
Where are the Dorian mothers
  That nurs'd thee for such things?

Gone—like a dream of glory,
  Like a ripple on the sea;
Like the names of the 'base million'
  That won Thermopylæ!'

'Tis not the pomp of numbers,
  Nor circumstance of State,
Nor treasury of Crœsus,
  That makes a people great!

Nor yet the cunning artist,
  Nor the merchant, nor the sage ;
Nor thunder of ' Demosthenes,'
  Nor Plato's golden page ;

But the strong and healthy purpose
  Of stalworth hearts and true,
Threaten what will—result what may,—
  Still to dare on and do.

Remember this, young Hellas !
  Thou hast toil'd—and thou art free !
And all we say of Sparta
  Our sons may say of thee !

But give up double-dealing !
  Despise inglorious art !
Trust to ' Lycurgus' ' discipline
  To play a Spartan part.

The Bell of Brinkbourne.

1840. FINISHED 1874.

' They came in their might,
With King Henry's right,
To turn Church lands to lay.'
Lay of the Black Friar: Don Juan.

In those wild times, when Harry's gruff command
Of monks and nuns catharticiz'd the land,
A little Priory embay'd in wood,
Shadow'd by frowning rocks, on Coquet stood:
So deep the dell in which its cloisters lay,
So deftly shrouded from the glare of day,
The strong marauder resting on his lance
Bent, from the cliffs above, a baffled glance,
And the belated traveller's eager eye
In useless speculation wander'd by.

Poor were its holy cells, though trimly dight,
Too mean for envy and too low for spite;
Slender its fare, but hospitably shar'd;
Fair was its fame—by no vile tales impair'd;
While richer saints and brotherhoods throve ill,
In local honour this continued still;
The happy owners of a black rood tree
Of Saxon date, and wondrous potency.

Known for its cures through all the country side,
The peasant's wonder, and the brother's pride.
But seldom then did plunder long evade
The Baron's license, or the Bord'rer's raid,
Fit for the fold, the pocket, or the pot,
Unless it prov'd too heavy or too hot.
The day was come when Brinkbourne's 'frères' must flee,
To wander outcasts under greenwood tree,
Or beg (for Mary's sake) from door to door,
Precarious shelter from her friends the poor.
Far other destiny, another fate
Did the first founder haply contemplate;
A gallant knight by late compunction led
To make in Coquet's dell his rocky bed;
And merit Heaven by scourge and thong, to die
In grievous doubt, and famous sanctity.
Mysterious offspring of those troubled times
When cowls could blot, and mortmain ransom crimes.
Yet who aright this brotherhood would paint
Must not dig down too deep into the Saint;
For Learning here went, as she did elsewhere,
With clouted shoon, and garment worn threadbare.
And pure Religion's evanescent ray
Linger'd not here to break again in day.
The doubtful worthy of whose deeds we've heard
Was the chief saint to whom their rolls referr'd,
And though the jealous guardians of his bones,
Henry declar'd, and many thought them drones.
To Pagan myths they lent a general aid,
For love of neighbourhood, and for good of trade;

With half the country side they counted kin,
Reliev'd their sickness or assoil'd their sin;
Their intervention stay'd domestic strife,
Rebuk'd the husband and consol'd the wife.
Their prayers and wise exorcisms best could stay
Th' offended ghost, and drive the fiend away;
Their jolly roundsmen begging twice a-year
Took news and blessing, and brought back good cheer.

And now they heard—how on a luckless day
The King had given their Priory away,
With twenty others, all of different sizes,
Some of them less, and others greater prizes,
To a great Northern Baron who had sworn
To leave no monks from Alnwick to Brinkbourne.
Close in the fastness of the dell they kept,
No truant foot beyond their threshold stepp'd,
In hope the storm that fill'd the darkening sky,
Might growl and thunder, but at last pass by.
'Twas sweet to hear the military mode
In which the Baron's riders ask'd their road.
Models they were of soldierly civility,
And cross-examin'd bumpkins with ability:—
As thus—'You gaping, staring, country louts!
Tell us the rascal friars' whereabouts!
For bluff King Hal has sworn by every martyr,
The pursy hypocrites shall catch a Tartar.'
The peasants lov'd the monks—the soldiers got
Directions where the Priory was not.
Accounts display'd such monstrous contrariety,
They 'gan to swear with infinite variety.

O'er hill and dale they spread in baffled search,
And found themselves at evening in the lurch
And a most tow'ring passion—when there fell
Full on the Captain's ear a pealing bell!
For Brinkbourne's monks, good souls, would celebrate
In jolly guise this lucky turn of Fate;
And Brinkbourne's Prior (not yet declar'd a winner,)
Caus'd brother Lawrence ring the bell for dinner.
These merrie notes (sad harbingers of woe)
Circled in tell-tale echoes from below.
Like Theseus led by Ariadne's clew,
Like Lion guided by the jackal crew,
Like him of death regardless as of damp,
Who trimm'd his midnight course by Hero's lamp,—
Down came the troopers—now they gain the door,
Now clank their belted brands adown the floor;
Curl their moustachios with heroic ire,
Flies from their soil'd array Northumbrian mire.
They call for drink—the rosiest monks turn pale,—
The Prior seeks counsel in a jug of ale,
And vainly strives the nut-brown draught to vary
With vows to all the Saints and Virgin Mary.
Business and supper now went hand in hand;
The monk's best Rhenish and the King's command.
So have I seen some graceless urchin's lip
The foaming porter's mantling treasure sip,
What time dark fears his mother's soul annoy,
Lest frightful accident detain the boy.
The shrine was stripp'd of gold and silver store,
The jewell'd pyx lay shatter'd on the floor:
The black oak chest hoop'd round with iron bands,
Flew open now to sacrilegious hands;

The founder's skull from its chas'd coffer rent,
Grinn'd on the ruin he could not prevent;
And priceless missals reverent and old,
Blazon'd with every tint, and rough with gold,
Like childhood's primer hopelessly forlorn,
Gap'd with their vellum leaves besmirch'd and torn.

Morning presents a scene of burly woe,
Forth on their way the pilgrim fathers go.
With novel toil their pursy bosoms heave,
Sometimes they halt for breath, sometimes for grief.
Like Romeo lingering near his Juliet, they
Return, and hesitate, and long to stay.
Anon they turn to gaze—for who can roam
An exile without one last look at home?
Where swell'd the anthem ribald jests prevail,
And brawling license clogs the lab'ring gale.
Within their buttery hatch where late they fed
The houseless poor with charitable bread,
The drunken trooper snorts in restless dream,
And foaming barrels pour a wasteful stream;
The Bell in happier days their simple pride
That cheer'd, and warn'd, and knell'd the country-side,
Hailing the infant to this world of pain,
Sounding the marriage peal of love-lorn swain,
At whose alarm the hardy Borderer rose,
And Bamborough's merrie archers drew their bows;
Whose solemn tones proclaim'd the fleeting breath,
When rev'rend age succumb'd in peaceful death,
Or manhood fell like hale and leafy oak,
Or childhood's flower was snapp'd by luckless stroke;—

Prepar'd with serious note, and merrie peal,
A call to matin song or evening meal;—
This bell came tumbling through the Convent door,
Trundled by roaring soldiers, quite a score.
The doleful clapper groan'd, and jarr'd, and creak'd,
The fathers told their beads, the Kelpie shriek'd! . . . .
With many a savage oath and bitter jest
By drunken wit in nameless words express'd,
In Coquet's blackest pool the bell they flung!—
Down Coquet's rocks the moaning echoes rung,
'Twas the last requiem from its iron tongue!

The walls have long been stripp'd—the garden shade
For evening nap or contemplation made,
Profan'd by stabled steeds gives shelter now
To roving herd of swine, or truant cow;
To buttery hatch no jolly monks repair,
The mullion'd windows without casements stare;
From moss-grown niches grimy saints look down,
With damag'd noses and a double frown;
From chapel roof banner and crest are torn,
And utter ruin has oppress'd Brinkbourne.

But still, as babbling age delights to tell,
Enshrin'd in rocky corner hangs the bell!
No envious rust impairs its silver tone,
No mosses clasp it in a verdant zone;
Around its sides the rushing streamlets glide,
Within its cup the water spirits hide:
For constant still in brawling Coquet's deeps
O'er his lov'd bell the Kelpie vigil keeps.

Still if ye plumb aright that depth profound,
The gloomy pool returns a tinkling sound.

The moral's of some use whate'er ye think it!
Keep your own secrets! Brew your ale and drink it!
Had these good fathers din'd without their bell,
They'd din'd less noisily but not less well:
Nor had they, like the cackling hen, betray'd
The snug retreat in which their egg was laid.

The Rhine.

1860.

FROM glaciers lone and desolate
  In icy rills I creep;
The shaggy pine my fosterer is—
  My nurse the snows a heap.
I give no promise of renown,
  I am neither broad nor deep.

But I have gather'd waters
  From many a nameless rill;
At every mile I meet a foe,
  And I am master still;
I turn all floods behind me
  In the fury of my will.

On to the wall of granite,
  The fool that threatens me!
A rib of Earth's grim skeleton
  Cast up for men to see:
Above, around, below I rave,—
  And once again I'm free.

On to the sable wilderness!
  On to the drouthy plain
That longs to suck my waters up
  Chill from the frozen main!
On with a load of forests
  That follow in my train;

Past many a splendid city
  Grown old in tale and song,
By many a dungeon tower, and keep,
  The ghastly tombs of wrong,
'Neath many a fretted minster spire
  That hath been honour'd long.

Now girt with immemorial pines,
  Now gemm'd with laughing isles,
Now frowning through a solitude
  Of threescore sombre miles;
Now breaking forth to light and life
  In plains where harvest smiles.

A moving water column
  Silent and strong as death,
I brawl not o'er my calling—
  I waste no peevish breath;
Place for the great! room for the strong!
  My voice imperious saith.

No rocks disturb my mastery,
  Nor wreck of stranded trees,
The only power that ruffles me

Is the steam-ship and the breeze:
Resistless might is with me,
I wander where I please.

The kings of many provinces,
Floods mighty in their day,
Rivers that drain the mountains,
Own my superior sway,
And do me homage as I pass,
And lose their names for aye.

Till Maintz beholds my bosom
Broad as an inland sea,
Eager to win the crown of vines
That Bacherach keeps for me,
As an Emperor circled by his Peers
I move triumphantly.

Rhine of a thousand heroes!
Rhine of true hearts and hands!
What are the vapid praises
Of Ocean's golden strands?
In me behold a thousand floods,—
And the love of many lands!

The peasant in his antique cot,
The Burgher ever slow,
The Noble from his falcon's nest,
The monk that sighs in woe;
The Bursch look fondly in my face,
And love me as I flow.

To Noble, Burgher, Merchant,
  My lavish hand brings wealth ;
To the poor I bring content and peace,
  For I do good by stealth ;
I please the eye, I lift the soul . . .
  Health to the Rhine then ! Health !

The Dark Hour.

1845. FINISH'D 1871.

THE friends of youth drop early,
  The friends of age come slow,
Time is a master surly,
  And years are fraught with woe!

Oh pleasant, pleasant were the dreams,
  And full of hope the hours!
When life was not what now it seems,
  Husks in the room of flowers.

A little day, a few more years,
  Some aspirations yet,
And the sun that bright with promise rose
  In utter gloom shall set.

And the place, alas! that knew me once,
  Shall see my face no more;
But the fool shall simper, and the dunce
  Shall blunder as before.

And plume himself on crudest schemes
 By happy chance repriev'd;
While I shall perish in my dreams,
 Nought conquer'd, nought achiev'd!

And yet I feel within me stir
 Good metal sound and true;
I am no green artificer
 With my craft to learn anew.

I cannot be so much mista'en,
 I do not lag behind;
I have not toil'd so long in vain!—
 No! 'tis the crowd that's blind.

Hush, soul! the man who scorns to cringe
 Shall never win a name,
Till death have oil'd the creaking hinge,
 And shot the bolts of Fame.

Of this let all men be assur'd—
 Honour deserts the man,
No matter by what claims allur'd,
 That fights without a clan.

Cæsar by legions unenforc'd,
 Or Cicero's silver tongue,
By friends and clients un-endors'd,
 May to the winds be flung!

The only bond that can enchain
   Success to living worth,
Is the suffrage of the dull and vain,
   And the cliques that govern Earth.

At last comes Death and rights the scale
   Of justice and of wit;
But fools that in their lives prevail
   Have all the best of it.

The Table d'Hôte.

1857.

May sigh to think he oft has found
His warmest welcome at an inn.

THE world is like a table,
A table at an inn.
Where some are always going out
And others coming in.

Here, where I sit, some Kaiser
Sat haply long ago,
While beneath him lay the Roman's dust,
And who knows whose below!

And where I sit shall maidens,
And young men, sires and mothers,
Sit in the misty dawn of years,
But to make room for others.

With hearts as warm as mine was
When first I saw Cologne,
With hearts as cold as mine is,
When now I see Cologne!

Sweep off the crumbs and fragments!
  Let the cloth be fresh and clear!
Leave no sign of the buried past,—
  The present is our sphere.

But whoever they were and whenever they liv'd,
  They were but flesh and blood!
And the same passions fir'd their veins
  That burn'd before the Flood.

And no matter for the polish,
  The world is still the same;
And call it by what name you will,
  Good is good—and sin is shame.

This is the broad distinction
  That must endure for aye,
Though lightnings wing the telegraph,
  And steam curtail the way!

Hence cross and decoration!
  Contemporary breath;
The tree of Fame's a mourner,
  And blossoms after death.

And amongst us yet may ponder
  Unnotic'd and unknown,
The man whose name posterity
  Shall marshal forth alone.

So was it once with Caxton,
With Luther and with Tell,
With Cromwell and with Washington,
And some few more as well.

And still the brave and loyal heart
Hath harder task mayhap,
Than 'Simeon of the Pillar' knew,
Or the monk that built 'La Trappe.

It is not maceration,
Nor self-impos'd restraint,
Nor border of phylactery,
But worth that makes a Saint.

And those whose wand'rings lead them
Where relics grow so rife,
Ask—were these men so holy
When they belong'd to life?

Or is this worship but a phase,
Another shape, I guess,
Of the Fish-God in Ashdod,
The scales of Heathenesse?

And not the natural weakness
Of sinners that adore
Whatever of the great and good
Hath travell'd on before?

Disdainful Anglo-Saxon,
One parting word with thee!
'Tis not thy vast irrev'rence
That makes thee great and free!

Visit these Gothic temples,
Be silent if severe,
Offend not where thou may'st not bow—
Nor where thou doubtest sneer!

With all thy vaunted knowledge,
There are more ways than thine,
In which a man may worship God,—
And each befits its shrine.

The Desert hath its simple prayer,
The glorious Dome its forms,
The prelate loves his mysteries,
The Puritan his qualms;

And the World is like a table,
A table at an inn;—
Then let no traveller going out
Offend one coming in.

'Neither Fear nor Hope.'

Motto of the Cardinal of Bourbon.

1860.

Ye that have seen the morning sun
  Without a cloud to blot
The splendour of his countenance—
  I say to ye—Hope not!

Ye that have seen the dawn of Love
  In palace or in cot,
And reckon'd on his mid-day beams,
  I say to ye—Hope not!

Ye that have builded airy towers
  Where festering marshes rot,
And thought betimes to dwell therein—
  I say to ye—Hope not!

Ye that have labour'd for renown,
  Fame without speck or spot,
The many's homage to the few—
  I say to ye—Hope not!

Ye that are guileless and sincere,
  Slaves of ye know not what,
A great man's word, a woman's wile,
  I say to ye—Hope not!

Ye whose beginnings were as Job's,
  Whose lines are fall'n with Lot,
Spoil'd children of a spendthrift star,
  I say to ye—Hope not!

And ye whose chance is desperate,
  Of every friend forgot,
Outcasts of charity and heaven,
  I say to ye—Fear not!

Put the broad shoulder to the wheel,
  Strip to it on the spot!
Wrestle another fall with Fate!
  Be steadfast, and fear not!

Full many an atmosphere of calm
  In tempests is begot;
Who knows how near yon quiet lies?
  Press on, then, and fear not!

The stormiest times and tides may be
  True portions of Love's plot;
Fame's auriole lights on haggard brows:
  Press onward, and fear not!

Keep the stern tenor of your way,
  Swerve not aside one jot!
Hope not—'twere better for your peace;
  But come what will—fear not!

The Queen and the Birds.

1857.

UPON a wild and sounding shore,
  Where stormy waves beat high,
There sat a Queen, and, what is more,
  A Saint condemn'd to die.

The rose had vanish'd from her cheek,
  But heavenly lustre shed,
Speaking as nought of earth can speak,
  A glory round her head.

And fair and floating were her locks,
  And white her lily hand
Contrasted with the sombre rocks
  And the dunes of driving sand.

She sat apart—she will'd it so—
  The salt spray damp'd her hair,
And sea-weed breezes faint and low
  Came drifting past her chair.

Watching her ebbing spirit's strife,
  The people stood apart,
That lov'd her for her saintly life,
  And the goodness of her heart.

They watched her as a mother's eye
Watches a dying child;
When she breath'd in pain no check was dry—
And when she smil'd, they smil'd.

And day by day, the little birds
Flew pleasantly to greet,
And in small showers settle down
And twitter at her feet.

They look'd into her friendly face,
And they were not afraid;
And without etiquette or place
A mimic court they made.

They perch'd in flocks upon her chair,
They had perhaps no claim;
They knew not why they nestled there,
But they lov'd her, and they came.

Yet the curse of Courts was in the air,
So lightly folly comes,
They quarrell'd for the chiefest share,
And fought for largest crumbs.

And it did her good to watch their strife,
And all their little ways;
She had seen enough of it in life,
Where there was less to praise.

One morn they sought the wonted spot,
Bright sunbeams warm'd the air;
They waited—but their Queen came not,
And empty was her chair;

And silent was the sandy lea,
And silent all the shore,
Save the moaning of the restless sea,
And the wild surge's roar.

The multitude had left the strand,
Hush'd was the voice of mirth;
There were many mourners in the land,
And one Saint less on earth.

The picture which suggested these lines was in the collection of Monsr. Vanderberghem at Brussels. It was painted from nature not long before the death of Louise Marie Queen of the Belgians.

She is represented sitting in a chair on the beach at Ostend, with the birds (an historical fact) round her.

It was impossible to look upon it without emotion.

The Landscape.

1840.

DEEP in the mellow West the sun was setting,
A wilderness of Eastern tints begetting;
The red clouds mantled o'er his sinking head
Like demons hovering round a good man's bed;
With envious pinions striving to obscure
Th' eternal light which shall the more endure.

Rippled adown the dell the brawling stream,
And echoed from the moor the curlew's scream,
The plashing trout, the water's drowsy fall,
The evening muir-fowl's monitory call,—
Such were the sounds, so soothing and so sweet,
That join'd in cadence to the traveller's feet.
And stunted birch and grizzled copsewood fring'd
The lower glen, but where the sunbeam ting'd
The bleak hill's shoulder shrub nor flower fair
Might bide the shrewd dint of the mountain air;
Save here and there appear'd a blasted trunk,
Its foliage wither'd and its column shrunk.
Alone in dismal solitude it stood;
The last survivor of some mighty wood
That grew, and flourish'd once, and pin'd, and fell,
And strew'd with giant wreck the wasted dell.

So 'tis in life—the many far and wide
Cluster around th' ignoble fireside,
And nestle them where'er a nook they find
To shelter cowards from life's withering wind :—
But yet some stubborn spirits strive with fate,
And hold with fickle Fortune stern debate,
Worsted but not subdued—as if to show
What, if he dar'd it, puny man might do.
Blasted and seared are they with many a scar,
Scath'd by the passion's internecine war.
These are the men on whose stern brow is plain
The fearful stigma God first set on Cain ;
That all should know him, fear him, shun his path,
As they would flee the lion in his wrath.
The paltry crowd beholds in servile awe,
The man who knows no weakness, owns no law ;
Forth on his way he goes, alone, unbless'd,
And like the cast-out spirit finds no rest.
None say, God speed thee ! none his mood gainsay,
Himself his guide, his counsel, and his stay ;
Wrapp'd in himself he craves no kindred mind,
In whose converse a passing joy to find ;
Nature made him and them for different ends ;
Men are the tools he works with, not his friends.
While others blended with the shadows lie,
He stands in broad relief against the sky,
As who would say—'Ye storms, thou burning leven,
Ye whirlwinds, voice of much-offended Heaven,
Here be your mark ! on me fall all your weight !
Make this heart sear, this bosom desolate !

Such were the men, the early Tragic Muse,
In verse severe throughout their weird pursues.
Prometheus bound, the vulture's living prey,
Owning his failure, scorning to obey;
His was the torment what he lost to know—
And railing comprehend th' abyss of woe.
Oh, tree of knowledge, evil was the hour
That twin'd thy dainty leaves in Adam's bower!
Thy mocking shade is poison, dust thy fruit;
And Death and Hell surround thy Upas root!

Such too the man that Heaven, for royal crimes,
Sent forth to conquer in these latter times.

The social world was springing to new life,
With many an untold wish and longing rife;
High aspirations yearn'd and valour spoke
Louder than law, and stronger than the yoke;
Dropp'd from the peasants' neck the feudal chain,
And left him foaming with remember'd pain.
A man alone there lack'd to strike the blow,
And he arose in fiery Mirabeau.
With cynic earnestness he flung aside
The myths of ages, and the rules of pride.
Then like a fairy vision disappear'd,
The house of cards by priests and courtiers rear'd.
And store of fools conventionally great,
Found that the breath they scorn'd could mar their state;
For full-blown pride, secure in pomp of place,
Mocks signs and wonders, and refuses grace.
Nor dream the rich that strong opinion lies,
Beneath the shepherd's frock of homespun frieze;

Yet so it is—that State no warning saves,
Where fools are masters, and wise men are slaves.
And so 'twas seen, when first resistless grown
The cap of liberty o'er-topp'd the crown;
And Reason reign'd—and Sieyes' impious hand
Scar'd Revelation from the godless land,
Made life a torment—flung a hopeless gloom
Around the dark suspicions of the tomb,
And bade each miscreant eat and drink his fill;—
Like Eve's first tempter, liberal of ill.

Then rose Napoleon, as a Comet's light
Breaks on some Eastern Sage's wondering sight.
Forth from the boundless realms of space he came,
Troubled his aspect, and his track all flame;
A man like none before him,—born to be
His age's wonder, scourge, and mystery.
He knew mankind, and scorned their feebler clay:
Sternly bade rivals tremble and obey.
They met his glance, confess'd the contest vain,
And sued for places in the Consul's train.
A morn of glory follow'd, scream'd and rose
The Gallic eagle o'er a score of foes;
And cast athwart the plains his bloodshot eye,
To choose the boldest for his enemy.
While ancient fools dozed o'er the art of war,
And hal'd the victor to their puny bar:
Unfetter'd he by prejudice or rule,
Sapped the foundations of their tottering school,
And rubbed from simple souls pedantic rust
By laying Empires in their own great dust.

Italian plains again receiv'd the Gaul,
Again he camp'd 'neath Rome's eternal wall:
But not as once did godlike forms dismay,
And well-nigh scare th' invader from his prey;
And no Camillus liv'd like him of old,
To bid expediency put up his gold.
Egypt's brute Gods their dusk complexions hid,
And centuries gaz'd from Cheops' pyramid;
Great Cæsar's fortune, Pompey's nobler shade
Hail'd to their stage, a greater pest self-made,
And Suns like theirs illum'd with angry ray
The opening splendour of Napoleon's day.
But see, the veteran's not unmanly woe,
Moistens with tears the adieus of Fontainebleau.
For Nations vast and many were combin'd,
To stay the soarings of one master mind;
And Winter's ruthless snows and Scythian hands
Had dealt destruction to his conquering bands,
Fond fools by love of him and glory led,
To win the honours of the nameless dead.
He came with nought but hope, and his good blade;
He goes with not so much—but ne'er shall fade
The wreath he wrought himself, nor droop the tree
He gave the French, and call'd it Liberty.
Its leaves were water'd by too many tears,
Its growth was foster'd by too many fears,
Its trunk was set in too much blood and woe,
Of friends and foes, to wither lightly so.

Behold yon point of rock! least though it be
Of the lone islands tenanting the sea,

There, had he once again his flag unfurl'd,
Like Archimedes he had mov'd the World;
And there, in meet seclusion humbly laid,
He rested 'neath the weeping willow's shade.
Vain was the boast and empty the display
That tore from thence his coffin'd dust away,
And broke the solemn quiet of his grave,—
(As if his glory could not pass the wave),
That Joinville's maiden sword might guard his urn,
And hollow Thiers proclaim his late return.
Can praise like this exalt a mighty name?
And is such mockery to pass for fame?

No, mightiest spirit! in whatever sphere
Smoulders the flame that blaz'd so fiercely here,
If that it smoulder—nor no more confin'd
Blaze forth exulting with its rays refin'd,
Bright as the stars we know not of, and clear
As spotless mornings of the early year:
Thine is no marble pomp, no sculptur'd bays;
These may remind where memory decays;
Thine is the Hero's monument, the page
That fires to glorious deeds an unborn age.
But if some other monument must be,
There is but one equivalent to thee!
Let prostrate Nations join in hateful toil,
And rapine raise, and blood cement the pile;
A mass like those where Nile's fat waters spread
Around the follies of the Memphian dead;
Then write an epitaph for all to see,—
That flesh is grass and Empire vanity.

Kossuth's Hymn.

1849.

IN the raven's gathering day,
In the bloody battle fray,
Hear us, when we fight and pray,
Hear us! when we're slain and slay;
God of the warriors of Arpad!

Come from lands where nations freeze,
Lena to Borysthenes,
Lapland to the Chersonese;
Swarming come like angry bees,
Foes of the warriors of Arpad!

Come, ye parasites of war,
Wolf and vulture come from far;
Here a thousand dainties are!
Feast on slaves of King, Czar,
Slain by the warriors of Arpad.

Hark! a peal of wild huzza-a-s.—
From thy throne above the stars,
Look upon the free Magyars,
Count their groans, and heal their scars;
God of the warriors of Arpad!

O'er the patriot's bloody grave,
Cause thy brightest flowers to wave,
Colours rare and odours suave
Doing honour to the brave,
  Fall'n in the battles of Arpad.

In a nimbus of delight,
Their free souls have taken flight;
O'er their bones we stand, and plight
Millions to the war of right;
  All of them children of Arpad.

Foul fall your unhallow'd speed,
Princes in our utmost need
'Gainst our liberties agreed;
What shall be your valour's meed?
  Graves by the wayside of Arpad.

Butt for every shaft of scorn,
Arms reversed and banners torn,
From the leaguer of Comorn,
Limps Ban Jellachich forlorn,
  Cursing the warriors of Arpad.

Nurs'd in every treach'rous art,
Austrian! take back thy dart,
Pointed at a Nation's heart!
Vengeance from the dust would start
  Were there no warriors of Arpad.

Hoc erat in Votis.

WIESBADEN, 1861.

YEARS, in whose history
  Wrinkles we trace,
Draw your sad furrows
  Light o'er her face!
Tenderly, slenderly
  Touch her fair brow!
Years, in whose mystery
  Old age sleeps now.

Shrink from endamaging
  Beauty so rare!
Grant her immunity,
  Spare her! oh, spare!
Smilingly, willingly,
  If it must be,
Let the change come o'er her
  Unseen by me.

Fair be the flight of ye,
  Wandering kings!
Seasons your chariot,
  Minutes your wings!
Years, in whose mystery
  Old age we trace,
Draw your sad furrows
  Light o'er her face.

Vingt Ans après.

WIESBADEN, AUGUST, 1861.

AND was it for those eyes of thine,
Of calm and saintly blue,
That I lost my share of hope divine?
On earth an outcast, too?

Is this the light whose beam excels
All other I have known?
Cold moon that brightens Ocean's cells,
To make them feel more lone?

Come, let us talk of what hath been,
And the lost past renew!
And hast thou prosper'd, my soul's queen?
Or hath thy life fail'd, too?

The storms, the calms, the days of strife,
Of reckless mirth and glee,
Have drawn their furrows o'er my life,—
What have years done for thee?

Hast thou been faithful to thy trust,
  And found no answering heart?
Dost thou deplore, as still I must,
  The fate that bade us part?

Thou answerest not! I like that best:
  Let Mystery shed her pall
O'er dreams that might not stand the test,
  And hopes I knew must fall.

'And after many Years we met.'

1856.

AND after many years we met,
  And she was all alone;
I look'd into her glorious face
  As one gazeth on a stone.

I spoke to her of trivial things;
  I listen'd to her voice:
Its music had no longer power
  To bid my soul rejoice.

The vision of my youth was flown,
  The silver chord was rent,
The wheel was broken at the fount,
  The strong delusion shent.

And yet it was the self-same form;
  The same lips spoke to me;
The same enchantress fram'd the spell:
  But my heart was dead, or free.

O Love! thou art a changeful thing!
  Had I once thought thee so,
I had never rav'd, and groan'd, and pin'd,
  And liv'd so long in woe.

Creature of fancy! fever'd dream!
  Child of a great mistake!
We deck an image for ourselves,
  And worship what we make!

Experience.

1856.

In the morning of youth,
  Down the river of life,
 How delightfully stealing we glide !
Our sails are all set,
And our hopes are all high,
 And we steer like the swan in her pride.

The worst that can happen,
The worst we need fear,
 Is a zephyr o'erburden'd with dew ;
Or the sunbeam that flings
O'er an innocent cheek
 A little more brown than its due.

No cares to annoy us,
No troubles to sour,
 Blithe hearts and exuberant health ;
What care we for honours ?
What reck we of State ?
 What are all the delusions of wealth ?

'Tis love that alone
Can embitter our hearts,
 From other disasters secure ;

But, alack for the day !
All the rest is child's play !
  He alone mocks at comfort or cure.

How pleasant, how taking,
How choice are his ways !
  What flowers in great handfuls he flings !
And stooping before him,
In hopes of his smile,
  Bows the wide world, from beggars to kings.

Alas for the lesson !
Alas for the woe !
  Alas, that such bright days should end !
But I tell to thy youth
Nothing more than the truth,
  I've tried it—be warn'd by a friend.

Alas!

1856.

Oh, the years! the pleasant years!
How trippingly they pass,
With their hopes and their schemes,
Idle deeds, and empty dreams!
Alas!

Oh, the years! the wretched years!
How haltingly they pass,
When disillusion's left
To souls of joy bereft!
Alas!

Oh, the days! the days of gold!
That shall never more return;
Buried dead and deep ye lie,
Pride of life, and lust of eye,
In Care's urn.

There's a dirge in every breeze
That filters through the fern;
Mourning voices choke the air,
Saying—'Weep for all that's fair!'
Weep and learn.

The Greenwood.

1840.

As I was alone in the greenwood one day,
I heard the birds carol from every spray:
Till one hopping down, in a pitiful tone
Sung,—'Why art thou here in the greenwood alone?'

'O bird! painted bird! my poor heart is not whole,
And the music of nature falls dull on my soul;
I feel not the sunbeams, I seek not the shade,
Since she that once lov'd me has wander'd and stray'd.'

'Ah! we saw thee last summer, and envied thy bliss,
No bower of our woodlands unblest by her kiss;
How her eyes used to glisten in rapture's full tide,
When she threaded our mazes with thee for her guide!'

'But she's gone, bird! she's gone, like the leaves of last year,
Like a minister's smile or a young widow's tear.
Then tell me, sweet bird, where thou sitt'st on the tree,
Hath the mate of thy bosom dealt truly with thee?'

'A tyrannous hawk, swooping down from the sky,
Pounc'd on her, poor fool! as she struggled to fly:
Oh, it grieved me to see, as I cower'd in the thorn,
The breast of my darling so mangled and torn!'

'And now, bird, thou wand'rest unheeding, like me,
The warmth of the sunbeam, the shade of the tree,
Fatiguing the echoes with pitiful moan;
'Oh, why am I here in the greenwood alone?''

'Indeed do I not!—what can sighing avail?
And life is too short for a true lover's tale;
I got me a new love the very same day,
And woo'd her, and won her, and bore her away.

'Then I rose from the bank where I lay in despair,
And I wrung from my heart the black drop that was there:
I got me a new love; and should she go too,
I'll get me another, however untrue.'

Annus Domini.

1856.

ONCE I was young,
As everybody was;
Once I was young, d'ye see?
And I made love,
As everybody did,
And they made love to me.

But the spring-tide pass'd—
Oh, why didn't it last?
It was such a joyous time;
And my locks grew grey,
And the raven's wing
Was silver'd o'er with rime;

And the sylphs I knew
In the former days
Grew graver, and broader, and fatter:
For with us all,
Both short and tall,
Annus Domini was the matter.

So I'm silent now
Where I whisper'd once,
And they listen'd smilingly.
For were to do as everybody I,
As everybody does,
They would not do so to me.

A Drinking Song.

SEPTEMBER, 1861.

DRINK! drink! drink
To the grape that crowns the bowl!
Drink! drink! drink
To woman that rules the soul!
The bowl that asks renewing,—
The woman that works our ruin;—
Pleasantly, surely,
Often demurely:
For the Goddess of Pleasure
Loves these above measure,
And trusts to their keeping her every treasure.
These are they
Who mean yes, and say nay!
And leave you to fill up the rest of the play.
Deep, deep they are; deep
As the ice-bound currents that roll
Where ocean monsters sleep
Far away, far by the Pole!
But never did monster in ambush there
Know less its pitiful prey to spare,
And never did Kraken its crest uprear
With less to follow and more to fear
Than these,
With the will to kill, and the power to please:—

Pleasing, and killing,
Their mission fulfilling,
Alternately burning, alternately chilling,
And ever finding their victim willing.—
Ah, me!
That such Sirens should be,
With their rocks cropping up upon every sea,
For the peril of man everlastingly;—
Toll his knell, toll!

But without them what were our life?—a blank,
A parlous void, a shipwreck'd plank,
Long and lazy, and dull and dank,
The least of the least, in the lowermost rank,
A thing for which we have none to thank:—
And the bowl?
Drink stoutly down from the beaded brim,
Where Bacchus's bubbles in purple swim,
And bathe thy lips till thine eyes grow dim,
And begone dull care with thy visage grim,
And welcome mirth, farce, folly, and whim,
Without control!
For never a man that drinketh fair,
But mocketh at grief and sorrow and care,
And the frowns of life, and the freaks of the fair,
And the ups and downs that all must share,
Chasing life's butterflies costly and rare
From pole to pole:
A weary chase with never an end,
A pitiful world without any friend,
Where all will borrow, and none will lend,

And sorrows to-day fresh sorrows portend,
And, bad as they are, things never will mend!
Then fill the bowl!
Wreathe it with roses,
This morn on the stem!
Nothing disposes
To drinking—like them.
Let the juice that mocks at sorrow
Banish reck'ning till to-morrow:
Reck'ning with ourselves or host,
Reck'ning that I dread the most.
Plunge thy brain in glorious wine,
Bathe thy lips in joys divine!
Take thy glass and give me mine,
And from every care of thine
Release thy soul!

Old and New.

FEBRUARY 22, 1844.

THE days, the days are gone
Of chivalrous emprise;
Of high deeds wrought for Ladies' love,
For light of Ladies' eyes.

And with them, too, is fled
The reverence and awe
That thron'd her high in gentle hearts,
And made her wish a law.

'Twas hence the Poet drew
The secret of his art,
'Twas this alone that tuned his lyre
Responsive to his heart.

It nerv'd the victor's arm amidst
The revelry of death;
It hung in failing accents
Upon the vanquish'd breath;

And every true knight moved
A goodly satellite,—
And shone not by his own,
But by his Lady's light!

Now hollow hearts and glozing tongues
  Are quit for light disgrace ;
And men must woo for money,
  And women wed for place.

To bear their heads the higher
  Amidst the giddy throng,
They sacrifice to Mammon,
  And do poor lovers wrong !

Come back ! come back, bright Surrey !
  Revisit this false scene !
And teach us all the tenderness
  That won thy Geraldine !

Prologue.

Written and spoken by the author at Newnham Paddox, in the character of Frederick, in 'The Youthful Queen,' February 1, 1844.

In days gone by, when, midst their other feats,
Men paid their Christmas bills and took receipts,—
Ere States regardless of their reputation
Invented that sad word 'Repudiation,'
And witty Sydney Smith, beguil'd to lend,
Forbade Republicans to call him friend!
But loudly roaring for his absent cash,
Denied—that those who took his purse stole trash:
When every man possess'd his household Jew,
Who cash'd his bills, should 'Hazard' or 'Maroo'
Frown for a time, and never nam'd security,
Trusting to Honour—then in all its purity:
In those Utopian times, so long since past,
Too bless'd for common use, too bright to last,
Plays had their prologues!—Long disuse, I know,
Has made them pass for bores, and reckon'd slow.
But there's no choice! so we who now appear
Before your stern tribunal sitting here,
Revive the dormant privilege, and pray
For much indulgence to our little play.

'Maroo.' Cockamaroo. A game much in fashion at the time.

'Tis for ourselves we ask, and not a bit
The author,—he must stand by what he's writ!
They tell me 'tis not bad, if we can act it,
And six years since not e'en 'The Age' attack'd it.

Should you be pleas'd with what you hear, accord
The grateful notice of a friendly word;
Be kind to faults that come, you don't know how,
Unless you tread the stage as I do now;
And midst your criticisms say, 'By Gad!
Look at that Frederick! he's not so bad.'

I'm bid to tell you, We employ few arts,
Our best performers those who know their parts.
Our scenes we're proud of—and you'll scarce believe,
They're vann'd from London and design'd by 'Grieve.'
Our dresses are our tailor's,—let him stamp
And grin like Genius of Aladdin's lamp,
Though duns prevail in these degenerate days,
Before three years, base is the slave that pays!
And since I'm here to chatter, let me not
Retire and leave you guiltless of the plot.
They charg'd me keep it secret, but I never
Could keep such things a moment,—did you ever?

Imprimis, Queen Christine, the Lord's Anointed,
Intends to marry, and is disappointed.
She, rising early on a Royal lark,
Stumbles on Frederick mooning in the Park,
Thinking on love, Cerito, and futurity,
Bank notes, light sovereigns, cash, and good security;

Inclin'd for marbles, sentiment, or slaughter,
Grill'd bones, and any beverage but water.

She falls in love,—for Love will not be rul'd,
Princes and peasants are alike befool'd.
Then comes the rough old minister—Lord save us!—
Who serv'd her Majesty's papa, Gustavus;
A virtuous statesman with a mulish will,
Who never cring'd for place nor robb'd the till,
And ne'er in forty thousand years had hit on
The tariffs and reforms that bless Great Britain.
His ministerial glance detects the evil,
He sees all Sweden going to the devil,
And like an old, unpleasant, useless brute,
Breaks off the play and marriage—*coûte que coûte*.

On this we hang some pleasant conservations,
Dialogues, solos, and recriminations,
With which we trust 'twill lie within our power
To make you pass a tolerable hour.

But stay! I must be off. 'Tis getting late,
And ladies never yet could bear to wait;
And though I'm ignorant she is the Queen,
I know she's charming, piquante, and sixteen.

Shall we, who crush'd their Fathers?

1844.

SHALL we, who crush'd their fathers
  At Crécy and Poictiers,
And bade their guard at Waterloo
  Be off, and clear the way,
Stand tamely by and tremble,
  When swords have left the sheath,
And Gallic threats are bandiéd
  In the British Lion's teeth?

Chorus.

'Tis thus they prate of honour,
  And spit upon the hem
Of Britannia's regal vesture,
  And shame her diadem.

No! by the sword of Edward—
  By the triumphs long ago,
Of the stout Norman lance
  And gallant English bow;
We will not cower before them
  While yet a bosom stirs
At the tale of Crispin's morning
  Or the Battle of the Spurs.

Chorus.

Their ships are rotting in our ports,
 Their banners deck our walls,
The tricolor is sighing
 In the breezes of St. Paul's;
For fear of us a hundred forts
 Gird Paris with a chain;
And the Jacobin and Anarchist
 Look on, and daren't complain.

Chorus.

They begg'd of us in sadness,
 And we granted to their plea.
The ashes of Napoleon
 From his prison in the sea.
We gave them all they asked for,
 But we could not give them back
The glory which departed
 When we thunder'd on his track.

Chorus.

The mark of England's heel
 Is branded on the neck
Of Paris and her citizens;—
 Of this they nothing reck;
But though her 'youth' may bluster
 And say, 'We felt it not!'
There is other 'youth' in England
 To make the brand as hot!

Chorus.

Then, Dupin, leave thy prattle,
And, Joinville, cease to write!
The Ancients had a custom
To draw their swords and fight.
Pray to the God of battles
For a stout heart and hand,
And a better sword than Hôche's,
To decimate our land!

Last Chorus.

And cease to prate of honour,
And spit upon the hem
Of Britannia's regal vesture,
And shame her diadem.

A parody on the above lines having appeared in *Punch*, marked by its usual ignorance and '*outre-cuidance*,' a little passage of arms was the consequence.

The '*Punch* writer' under the signature of 'Jenny Wren,' took exception to the pronunciation of the word Poictiers, which he said should rhyme with 'ears.'

John Davis, therefore, taking up his friend Maidstone's quarrel, wrote the following letter:—

'TO PUNCH.

Most mighty and crooked,—

If your friend 'Jenny Wren' cannot better her French,
Take a bit of advice, and get rid of the wench!
For your nose, dearest Punch! cannot carry off ears
That detect nothing wrong in the sound of 'Poictiers.'

Most mightily crooked,—

Allow me to take this opportunity of renewing to you the assurance of my distinguished consideration,

'JOHN DAVIS.'

FUGA IN AGRO EBORACENSI.

The Flight into Yorkshire.

(SUGGESTED BY LORD ELLESMERE'S DISMAL LETTER TO THE 'TIMES.')

Air—'Lord, how bright a day!'

JANUARY 4, 1848.

An old gentleman, reading the 'Times' *as he takes his constitutional walk, soliloquises as follows.*

IF it's all meant he says,
Run away, 'prentices!
Push along, draymen! cut away, Guards!
Make haste, my pretty dears!
Frenchmen love women's tears!
Nothing the 'Flight into Yorkshire' retards.

More of those 'new police!'
Stoppages will increase,
When we're all cutting and running, by Jove!
Help that old Lady there,
With her legs in the air!
Give poor Lord Brougham a pro-gressional shove!

There goes Lord Ellesmere!
There goes his Lordship's rear!
  Little the Frenchmen will see of him now.
There go the 'Bar' and 'Bench!'
There goes a pretty wench!
  All of them huddled together, nohow.

'Letter A., help me, pray!'
'Sorry, Marm! must say nay;
    Orders received, Marm, from ''Spector' Malone;—
Says, Marm, that them he calls—
Such were his words, Marm—Gauls,
    When they've once drubbed us will let us alone.'

There go the House of Lords!
There goes a 'gent' in cords!
    Who is the party that won't be denied?
'Tam's' representative,
Making a tentative,
    Out of the struggle to sniggle aside.

Spirits are sinking fast!
Sure, there's a tap at last;—
    Let us turn in there for courage to fly.
Now my throat's wetter, man,
I'm a deal better man.
    Come on then, Joinville, and have at your eye!

Britons, my lads, so rough!
Are ye such paltry stuff?
    Pliant and bending as willow-tree wand?

Let me see him whose hand's
Idle when Frenchman lands;
    Let me see him, I say, ducked in a pond!

Boasting and bullying
Disbelieve fully in!
    These are no weapons for Britons to wield!
Strong arm and heavy hand,
These shall defend our land,
    Though they be trained in no Algerine field.

Look at 'La Vendée,' then!
Raised she much better men?
    Were they more brave than the best of our sons?
Still, though a handful, they
Fought it out manfully;—
    Swords to artillery, cudgels to guns.

But if we find a rent
In our old tried garment,
    Shall we describe it, and point to it, too?
That, my Lord Ellesmere,
Seems to me very queer;
    And not so wise a plan as it is new!

Wild are our winds and tides!
Where our Queen's navy rides,
    Many a fleet would look strangely forlorn.
Flaunt away, Tricolor!
Braggart and safe-ashore!
    Ere one gets here shall a thousand be torn!

'Where is Joinville?'

DIALOGUE BETWEEN M. GUIZOT AND ECHO.

'MORNING POST,' DECEMBER 30, 1852.

'Hyla! Hyla! omne sonabat
Littus,' &c. &c.

GUIZOT.

WHERE is Joinville? Echo, say!
Where is Joinville?

ECHO.

Stol'n away!

GUIZOT.

Tell me where he now resides,
Where his '*boarder's beard*' he hides;
He, the nautical 'blow-hard,'
He, the conqueror unscarred
Of redoubtable Tangier:
He, the savage pamphleteer,
Advocate of pike and gun,
Louis Philippe's warlike son!

'*Boarder's beard.*' See the Prince de Joinville's pamphlet on the readiest way of annoying the English in case of war. He specially recommends 'boarding' at the earliest opportunity. Considering the many courtesies and politenesses that had passed between the Orleans family and Queen Victoria, some people thought Joinville's pamphlet *mauvais genre*.

Master of the game of jaw,
Advocate of clapper-claw,
Captain of the '*Lovely Hen*,'
When didst see him, Echo? When?

ECHO.

'Tother night, at half-past ten!

GUIZOT.

How, good nymph, was Joinville dress'd?

ECHO.

In his Admiralty best;
Cross of Honour, and cock'd hat,
Spurs, red breeches, and all that.

GUIZOT.

Prithee, where was Joinville going?

ECHO.

Where? Why not where gales are blowing
Fools to 'locker of old Davy;'
He was off to raise the Navy.

GUIZOT.

Pooh! dear Echo, let him bide!
He'll not hurt himself this tide!

Name of the frigate, *La Belle Poule*.

To Punch.

JULY 15, 1852.

WHEN first you came out, Punch,
With your jolly nose and hunch,
You were pleasant as 'Joe Miller' could desire;
But twenty-two years o'er,
We dismiss the rampant bore,
Nor look to gather roses from a brier.

Where's Doyle, your great adjunct?
And Thackeray? Defunct!
And A'Beckett?—made 'a beak'—alack, 'tis pity!
You've quarrelled with the men
Of the pencil and the pen,
And now you're neither popular nor witty!

Week by week we search and sigh,
And ask the reason,—'Why
Is Punch such remarkably dull reading?
Where's the wit that gave no pain,
And the merry rattling vein,
And the pleasantry that savour'd of good breeding?'

We read you, to be sure,
For the love that will endure
Of the days when you charm'd us above measure;
But a donkey's driv'lling in
The mangy lion's skin,
And lashing out, and braying there at pleasure.

Your 'bon-mots' might be claim'd,
And your portraits must be nam'd,
And your puns are as pompous as the 'Times;'
Your jokes require a key,
And your facts credulity,
And your verses flow and fancy, point and rhymes.

And your present motley pack,
With one hand behind my back
I can thrash, and think less of it than 'Percy.'
So put on better men
When you tackle me again,
For I'll neither show nor trouble you for mercy.

And whether you expire
In 'the Deluge' or the fire,
Or, by usual fate of bores, suicide,
Rest assur'd the public never
Pardons slang that isn't clever,
Or satirists found wanting when they're tried.

To Punch.

MR. PUNCH ! Mr. Punch !
Most exquisite homunch !
With your conk and your hunch,
Though you gabble on, and grunch,
'John Davis' for his lunch
A dozen such would scrunch,
And think nothing of the bunch.
So mumble on, and munch,
But be civil, Mr. Punch,
To JOHN DAVIS !

The Three Hoaxes.

'MORNING CHRONICLE,' NOVEMBER 22, 1851.

YOU very merry sportsmen, that live by cutting capers,
I pray you leave off hoaxing and joking in the papers!
Three 'stunners' in a fortnight—and each of them believ'd a week!
The '*rats and owls*,' 'the boa and rug,' and last 'the Palmerstonian freak.'

'Twelve rats were cramm'd with truffles, to give them greater stamina,
And the 'crammer' and 'the crammed' were both swallow'd by th' 'Examiner.'
Two owls were set to peck at them, with more or less malignity;
Against the Peace of Paris, and the press—its crown and dignity.'

'*The rats and owls.*' Towards the end of the year 1851, one of the most ridiculous hoaxes that ever was penned appeared in the shape of a communication from Paris:—

'The long-talk'd-of fight (says this prodigious document) between Lord H.'s two owls, 'Ironbeak' and 'Young,' and twelve rats, came off at midnight in the drawing-room of the Jockey Club. In the course of the fight, Prince Petulant, *alias* Chamouski, Rodilard, *alias* Vagabond, and Brilliant, *alias* Cut-Knuckles, fell together upon Young,' &c. &c.

One would think 'the blague' sufficiently patent; but the *Examiner* newspaper, afraid of letting such an opportunity slip, delivers itself of the following reflections on what it is pleas'd to call—

'A HORROR.'

'We hear 'the canaille' of Paris often spoken of, with disgust and horror of their brutal propensities, but if we may judge from an account now before us, the worst

And who, in spite of decency, did really make this match so queer?
Produce the truffles, find the rats, and bring all to the scratch? A peer
For H. must stand for 'Hertfordshire,' or 'Hertford,' ev'ry inch, Sir,
As sure as F. means '*Fonblanque*,' or '*Forster*,' at a pinch, Sir.

Well! Is it come to this indeed, that Sunday Censors Morum
Can't smell a rat, or nose an owl, with trash like this before 'em?
If they're so very gullible, why let 'em be less clamorous!
Although 'tis plain they never were of 'Upper Houses' amorous.

No sooner had this silly hoax in merry guise exploded,
Than down came joker 'number two' with his second barrel loaded:
''The 'Boa Zoological' had eaten up his rug in dreams,
Instead of the black rabbit that was wrapp'd up in it snug, it seems.

'canaille' in Paris, the most inhuman and perverted, is to be found in the aristocratic society of the Jockey Club of Paris.'

Here follows 'the blague' *in extenso*. Then come the comments.

'The law has no punishment for cruelty of this sort, but it should be signally punish'd by society. Who is this Lord H. who devoted his noble birds, born on his estate, to feast the appetite for cruel excitement, who saw the eyes of one eaten out of his head, and heard its dying scream under the torture of a horrible wound? Does he wear one of the highest tokens of the favour and honour of the Crown? Is the Garter a rat-killer's badge?'—*Examiner*, Nov. 8, 1851.

Next week came the leek-eating part of the business.

'Misled by the description of the aristocratic amusements of the Jockey Club of Paris, we threw out an insinuation which was unwarranted. Lord H., we are assur'd, has nothing to do with the Club in question, and has, moreover, been in England for the last month.'—*Examiner*, Nov. 15, 1851.

How pleasant it is to think that Mr. Albany Fonblanque—the great Whig Sachem—the bilious Editor of the bitter *Examiner*, should have the luck to fall into such a snare as this! Why not make the inquiry before writing the article? But the wish was father to the thought.

'And though the Serpent in his sleep pronounc'd the entrée charming,
The knot grew quite stupendous, and the consequence alarming;
Until a smart young watchman, who happen'd to pass by just then,
Pull'd out the blanket, half devoured, and set the critter free again!'

I would we had this blanket wherever household bore is,
To stop his mouth with woollen folds, and 'burke' his prosy stories.
But just thus much I've got to say about the present prank—it's
A well-known fact, i' the Regent's Park, the Boas have no blankets.

So now we come to 'hoax the third,' design'd with most audacity,
Which charges on a Noble Lord unparallel'd loquacity.
Says he,—'We've got our Kossuth out by moral tricks and scolding,
And, though I say it modestly, "judicious bottle-holding."

'As fast as ever you sent up addresses warm from Brummagem,
I packed 'em off by steam and rail,—I didn't stay to rummage 'em!
I sent 'em to "Sir Stratford" straight, with orders for disposing
Beneath the Sultan's very nose this mass of power imposing.

'"Twas thus we freed our Kossuth, and brought him here a jolly guest,
And of all the speakers that I know, he trims Imperial folly best.'
So thus concludes 'the third hoax,' and I trust we shall not see
The pleasant series ended with the mystic number Three!

JOHN DAVIS.

The Coup d'État;

OR, 'SHOOT! NEIGHBOURS, SHOOT!'

'JOHN BULL,' DECEMBER 13, 1851.

WE are Generals Cavaignac, Lamoricière, and Changarnier!
  And I am little Thiers, who wrote romance and call'd it history!
We were in, but now we're out, and pack'd off snug to 'Ham' away:
  So thus concludes our little plot, our *rubber*, and our mystery.
    Chorus.—Shoot! neighbours, shoot! All Paris is a-shooting now.
      Order, right, and anarchy are claw to claw.

I am 'Mons[r.] Morny,' that set the little trap for them;
  And I have brought it to this point,—'Does Paris care a rap for
    them?'
We are Representatives (at five-and-twenty francs a-day),
  And I am Léon Faucher! will no one take me up, I say?
      Shoot! &c. &c.

'*Our rubber.*' Chiefly by the contrivance of the Comte de Morny, the Generals Lamoricière, Cavaignac, and Changarnier, were secur'd; as was also Mr. Adolphe Thiers, who flattered himself he could play all parties round his little finger. He (Mr. T.) was said to have been engaged in a rubber of whist when he was taken and pack'd off to the Castle of Ham.

I am General 'Loewestine!' I order the Guard National
 To stay at home and mind their shops like Pères de Famille rational.
We are the 'Red Citizens,' who think bloodshed no crime at all;
 And we the famous 'barricades' that wouldn't do this time at all.
 Shoot! &c. &c.

I am Cato! (Louis Blanc), in London town I write away,
 And, stern as he of Utica, entreat my friends to fight away.
We are the 'Refugees' that sign'd our names his letter to;
 And I am 'Bertrand Clubbiste' who think that 'Blanc' had better go.
 Shoot! &c. &c.

I am the 'Montagne!' I feel a little flat just now;
 And we are the 'Departments' who can't think what you're at just now.
We are 'the Legitimists!' for 'right divine' that wrangle can;
 And we,—'burk'd correspondents of daily papers Anglican.'
 Shoot! &c. &c.

I am the 'Press!' I can't get in a word indeed;
 Nor tell the Public what I think; nor even what I've heard indeed.
I am 'La Demoiselle France!'—an unprotected Lady, Sir!
 And we,—discarded 'Orleanists' with reputations shady, Sir!
 Shoot! &c. &c.

'*I am Cato.*' 'Mr. Louis Blanc' did not do much for his own reputation upon this occasion. Indeed, he imitated, almost to the letter, the example of the great 'Jean Bon St. André' (treated of by Canning in his Anti-Jacobin verses), 'who fled full soon on the first of June, and bade the rest keep fighting.' A tiresome Communist, call'd 'Bertrand Clubbiste' (whether a nom de guerre or not I cannot say) put Mr. Louis Blanc into considerable difficulties, at a Leicester Square re-union of the Communist Committee of Safety, that sat in London to keep its brains the clearer. He bluntly said, 'Instead of making fine speeches, why don't you go?' The great Blanc turn'd white at the mention of such an eventuality, wondered at the ingratitude of men, and stayed where he was.

Hold! 'I'm Napoleon!' 'Six millions' made me President!
You took me for a trav'ller, 'Thiers!' I mean to be a resident!
'*Homme nul*' as you describ'd me once, henceforth I give the part up,
And now (like Brutus) drop the 'fool,' and take an Emp'ror's
heart up.

Shoot! &c. &c.

'*Homme nul.*' Mons[r]. Thiers, who thought political personages existed only by his permission, assur'd a friend that Prince Louis Napoleon (whom he had engaged in conversation) was of no account in the political calendar. 'C'est absolument un homme nul, mon cher!' What a conceited little man Thiers was! and what a weight of harm he did the State by the mixture of intrigue, and misstatement of historical facts, which put together made up his literary and political character. Nothing in his life became him so well as the activity he show'd in the endeavour to gain some terms for his country in the war of 1870. He is call'd by enthusiastic Frenchmen, 'Le liberateur de notre territoire;' but that title applies with more justice to Baron Rothschild and the rest of the Jews who found the 'three hundred millions' wanted, at no great loss to their own pockets. Since France was fined these 'millions' it is wonderful to think how much a pleasanter and more sensible member of the European family she has become.

The Count de Chambord.

1851.

'The Count de Chambord has begun to bestir himself lazily like a Bourbon.'—(*Our own Correspondent.*)

COUNT DE CHAMBORD (*sitting in an easy chair*).

ZOUNDS, an émeute! siége—Paris, blood, and 'fracas!'
Order my . . . pen and ink, and send for 'Blacas!'
Legitimacy's up! I'll not impede it!
I'll . . . write a letter and my friends shall read it!
Could 'Henri Quatre' do more?

Enter the LORD CHAMBERLAIN.

'Sire, all's prepar'd!
The pen is ready dipp'd, the paper air'd.'

Letter to Prince Schwartzenberg, &c. &c.

'Nous, Henri Cinq,'—No! that sounds somewhat formal!
'Dear Prince! the wretched state of things abnormal
In suffering France has gathered to a head;—
Napoleon's spoken out! disorder's dead!
The Assembly's kick'd, the Socialists are muzzled,
"Thiers" is checkmated, everybody's puzzled!
Generals well up in war's Algerian raps
Are taken out of bed in their nightcaps,
And spite of bluster, threats, and reclamation,
Pack'd up, and off to the next railway station.

The troops have acted (on the whole) like trumps;
There's been—('twixt you and I)—some heavy thumps.
In these I see, and I've great observation,
As you know, Prince, my speedy restoration.
'Louis' (like Monck) once seated will lay down
At my anointed feet the Bourbon's crown.
While thousands, sick of the electoral urn,
Will hail, with loud acclaim, their king's return.
All this will Louis do——and I!—well, I
Shall give him thanks and an indemnity.
But don't you think the time for action's come?
Roll in their car the Ban's Croatian drum!
That pleasant sound 'Legitimacy' loves,
Better than Jews love pelf, or Venus doves.
Strike in, dear Prince, 'twill hasten the transaction,
And bring my lazy party into action.
Checkmate Napoleon! and with him the Nation!
Accept, dear friend, my high consideration.'
&c. &c.

Palace of Prince Schwartzenberg. Enter the PRINCE'S JAGER.

Sir, by your leave, the Duke de Blacas 's come.

PRINCE.

Let him come in!

DUKE DE BLACAS.

'Great Sir, I bring you some
Important tidings, which my Master sends
To you direct, as to his best of friends.

He thinks the time for action 's drawing nigh,
And begs assistance from your sympathy.'

[*The Prince muses as he reads.*

' Hum ! 'Coup d'État !' and Constitution new !
Bay'nets again ! ' veut il s'asseoir dessus ?'
Still, he's the ruler and commands the army.
Duke ! ' autrement vois tu, nous serions charmés ?'
Louis has shown decision, pluck, and head,
Yet ' Henri ' thinks to govern in his stead.
Duke ! Let me tell you fairly we can't stir
In this affair, lest something worse occur !'

[*Exit Duke not a little surprised.*

Letter from the COUNT DE CHAMBORD *to the President of the French Republic.*

Dear Prince,
We greet thee, and of every move,
Up to this date, most cordially approve.
The ' coup d'état ' and subsequent arrests
Were (on our soul) exceeding merry jests.
No man's a hero in his nightcap ! t'aint
Becoming to the sinner or the saint.
You had the laugh !—that dish'd them ! for a fool
Alone can stand the force of ridicule.
The ' Red Republicans ' and Social beasts
(Stained with the bloody fare of Reason's feasts),
Like ' *King Anarchus* ' have been bound by force,
And made henceforth ' poor criers of green sauce.'

Up to the date of our own correspondent's letter no answer had been received from the President.

' *King Anarchus.*' King of the Amaurots. He was dethroned by Pantagruel, and made to cry ' green sauce.'—*Rabelais*, book ii. chap. 31.

Th' Assembly—wasn't that a pretty set?
With Cromwell's 'Take away that bauble!' met,
Has sunk to well-earned insignificance,
And passed away amid the jeers of France.
All parties, tired of their besotted pranks,
Held them too dear at '*five-and-twenty francs.*'
The busy workman, and the man of trade,
Who sigh for order and detest parade,
The farmer, soldier, priest, and artisan,
In short, each sound and valuable man
Throughout the State, in confidence takes breath,
Freed from prospective horrors worse than death.
So now to business without waste of ink!
You know, 'mon Prince!' that we are 'Henri Cinq,'
Last of the Bourbons, and though long away,
Still in our country's heart 'Le Desiré.'
Be great! be just! be loyal! and restore
The battered crown so many monarchs wore;
And for thyself accept—our good intention;
Free pardon, rank, and 'promise' of a pension.

JOHN DAVIS, 1851.

'*Too dear at five-and-twenty francs.*' The representatives of the Constituencies enjoy'd, by law (and in many cases it was said to be their chief object in choosing a political career) a salary of five-and-twenty francs per diem. There is no saying how many patriots and firebrands are unequal to the task of refusing such a pittance.

The Two Noodles.

A PAGE OF MODERN HISTORY.

'MORNING POST,' NOVEMBER 12, 1849.

THERE was a Prince in Germany,
  And many called him fool;
And passing idiots were the tribes
  So long that brook'd his rule.

His shrewd repressive minister,
  That cauterised to heal,
Kept folks in darkness (forty years),
  By lead, and cord, and steel!

One morn the wretchèd bubble burst,
  No minister was there;
No poor 'Old Noodle' twirl'd his thumbs
  In 'Vienna's' easy chair.

The game was up: the post-horses
  (Though German) gallop'd quick.
To 'Tyrol' flies 'Imperial Frantz'
  To England 'Metternich!'

With a grand crash the system fell—
  As I have seen a load,
In former coaching days, upset
  By donkey on the road.

'Old Noodle' drops the tangled reins
  He guided with disgrace,
And to the box of honour mounts
  'Young Noodle' in his place!

Germania! thine's a luckless chance,
  For whosoever rules—
Kaiser or patriot, king or churl—
  'Tis but a change of fools!

The Russian came from Poland's plains,
  And far Siberia's frost;
The Russian lent his 'Cossack hordes,'—
  The 'Russian' paid the cost.

The 'Russian' tamed the wild 'Magyar'
  Upon the Russian plan;
The Russian, though an autocrat,
  Did quit him like a man.

And when the war was over,
  The 'Russian Czar' did say,—
'"Young Noodle," take thine empire back:
  Let mercy rule the day!

'Bye-gones should pass! but study now
  Thy country's woes to heal;
Tear from thy book the bloody page
  Of cord, and lead, and steel!'

Young Noodle looked on sulkily,
  As child forbid to spin
A nasty great black cockchafer
  Upon a thread and pin.

Warriors of Arpad who had driven
  Croatia's Ban to fly,
In fest'ring batches hang unshriven,
  Or bullet-riddled die !

Pull up ! pull up, 'young Noodle !'
  And light your lamps, I pray ;
'Tis a dark road you travel,
  With donkeys in the way !

L'Empereur est Mort!

'GENTLEMAN'S MAGAZINE,' APRIL 2, 1873.

OF scourge and thong how sore's the need!
Back, yelping curs of 'Rochefort's' breed!
Back, sons of Communistic greed!
E'en bow the head!
From all your treacheries he's freed—
A great man's dead!

His faults, mayhap, were not a few,
But loyal were his aims and true;
He fail'd, as most French rulers do;
But he loved France.
While you, ye fickle, yelping crew!
Ey'd him askance.

From first to last, from great to small,
Who rightly answer'd Duty's call?
But 'Nemesis' prepar'd his fall,
While yours lack'd point;
Base, creeping maggots! bred in all
Times out of joint!

To him was given, perhaps, no right
For which your chivalry will fight;

But he found France in woeful plight,
With none to speed,
Long past the cure of words polite,
And did a deed.

He found her outrag'd and forlorn—
The shuttlecock of every scorn,
The waif of a late 'schemer,' born
Of her old kings:
And dar'd to promise her a morn
Of better things.

And had you rallied round him then,
With heart and hand, with sword and pen,
Ye puny sons of better men!
France had been sav'd.
Instead of this, the Lord knows when
Fools worse behav'd.

Your nobles long'd for kings gone by,
That bruisèd reed your 'bourgeoisie,'
For everything that pleas'd the eye,
Or fill'd the purse;
There was a talk of Liberty,
That specious curse!

With every principle mislaid,
With every rule of right gainsaid,
With every office made a trade,
The Press a trap,
The nation muzzled and betray'd—
What worse could hap?

He gave you order ; gave you, too,
A lost prestige built up anew ;
For, in a word, he govern'd you
Wisely and well ;
And History, if her page speak true,
Will one day tell—

Of Italy from slav'ry freed,
Old foes in amity agreed,
And Commerce in her utmost need
Reliev'd from wrong :
He could not check official greed,
That was too strong.

What were his crimes let others say :
A desp'rate game he had to play ;
And much he did in his short day
To curb the pranks
Of rogues that on fat burghers prey,
And got small thanks.

Then, sudden as an April shower,
Did faction paralyse his power,
And rivals rave, and liegemen cower,
And one and all
Left him, the scapegoat of an hour,
Alone to fall.

Embitter'd end of chequer'd part !
Ambition ta'en for whatthou art,

The wreck of feelings, soul and heart:
 Who would compete
For the best prizes of thy mart
 Laid at his feet?

But this I'll say of him,—although
He'd plumb'd the depths of weal and woe,
He never persecuted foe
 Or cast off friend.
Can any of his judges show
 Much less to mend?

In troubled times his star appear'd,
On 'Chaos'' self his throne was rear'd;
And yet for many a day he steer'd
 Through channels dark,
Till treach'ry's sunken rocks were near'd—
 They sank his bark!

Where there is no Love.

1860.

'For a crowd is not a company, and faces but a gallery of pictures, and talk but a tinkling cymbal, where there is no Love.'—BACON'S *Essays*.

A CROWD is not a company,
  Where there is no Love!
And talk but a tinkling cymbal,
  Where there is no Love!
And like a picture gallery
  In cold procession move
The faces of a multitude
  Where there is no Love!

What boots the smile of beauty,
  The cooing of the dove,
The ways that youth calls pleasant,
  Where there is no Love?
Where souls are not illumin'd
  With sunshine from above,
And hearts beat not in unison,
  And there is no Love!

The flowery bank, the vine-clad bower,
  The deepest, shadiest grove,
Are barren as the wilderness,
  Where there is no Love!

And friendship is but flattery,
  A faded wreath, a glove
That men cast off at pleasure,
  Where there is no Love!

Then cause me not, kind Heaven,
  Through this bleak world to rove,
Bewilder'd in the solitudes
  Where there is no Love!
Take from me power and riches!
  Snares of which most approve;
But hide me not, I prithee,
  Where there is no Love!

Bright's Speeches on the Crimean War made easy.

SAYS Bright, the belligerent Quaker,
In his 'Brummagem' ales and his cups,
'Whatever is 'ups' should be 'downs,' Sir!
Whatever is 'downs' should be 'ups!'

'Come tell me, ye Norman rough-riders!
Sleek aristocratical pups!
What good has this Russian war done us?
Has it multiplied turnips or tups?

'There's a hundred good thousands gone from us,
Young bachelors, able—that's why
A hundred fair thousand poor spinsters
In single misfortune must die!

'I cannot imagine two millions
Of millions—can you, my dear friends?
What sort of a bird 'tis to look at,
Or where it begins and it ends!

'And yet, I know who has got hold on't,
And who has spent every 'mag;'
The dark Norman Paupers you wot of
Have stealthily swallow'd 'the swag!'"

'"Tis gone, like the 'Western Bank swindle!'
This wealth of the mine and the loom!
The workman gets nothing but trouble,
And leave to rot out in the gloom.

'"Twas wanted to pet and to pamper
'The great territorial thief!'
'The balance of power' they call it!
I call it 'his out-door relief!'

'But this is not all, nor the worst on't!
For 'sucklings' like me, my belov'd!
Ever walking in wisdom and prudence—
Are horribly hustled and shov'd!

'Few men are politer than Russell!
To none he's politer than me!
And yet in the popular bustle
We seldom or ever agree!

'Good signs in a rising revenue
(At Liverpool prattling) he spied;
While I, for my life, cannot see it,
Though I open my eyes rather wide.

''Tis all very well for one born to
Enjoy a tight share of this wealth;
But how do 'the million' enjoy it?
Why, just as poor souls do—bad health!

'I don't like these thumping revenues!
  I'd rather by half they were small;
I don't like this fighting and squabbling!
  I don't like this truckling at all!

'I don't like this 'sanctified humbug!'
  I don't like this hitch in Reform!
And I hate every sort of bad weather,
  Unless I preside o'er the storm!

'I hate a 'a small family party,'
  And loathe every banker that croaks;
And detest every wheel in the parish
  That don't come to me for its spokes.

'And though I am told of the greatness
  Of England, its Empire, and Crown,
I hate all the trappings of serfdom—
  And wish they may shortly go down!

'In short, I love nothing but quarrels,
  And ledger-books dotted up right!
For whatever is 'ups' should be 'downs,' sirs!
  And the chiefest of 'downs' now is Bright!'

Oh where, and oh where!

(ON MR. BRIGHT'S RETIREMENT FROM PARLIAMENT TO RECRUIT HIS HEALTH.)

Tune—'The Little Wee Dog.'

OH where, and Oh where, is my little dog gone?
Oh where, and oh where is he?
He is gone to the land of the deer and the grouse,
And eke of the Salmonidæ!

And I wish in mine heart that my dog may catch
Very large fish, d'ye see?
Instead of playing with Ireland 'Old Scratch,'
A promising land so free!

L'Impresario.

About 1852.

'Dreading the deep damnation of his 'Bah !''
BEPPO.

In these prodigious times, when 'Joinville' writes,
And Yankee rogues, and Spanish Dons fly 'kites,'
And Frenchmen swear that Monsieur Abd-er-rahman
Shall hang, for shelt'ring 'Kader,' high as Haman ;
When 'Pritchard,' 'Pomare,' and Otaheite
Are like to furnish a long-winded treaty ;
When 'Warner's' shell's pooh-pooh'd,—'twill scarcely do
To take for theme poetical a Jew ;
And yet I must, dear Public! or the man
Will strip thee, next year, naked—if he can.
Ah, 'Sue !' thou'st lately gobbled the '*Erratic*,'
So I must starve upon 'the Operatic.'

When all his hireling scribes combine to tell
How 'Lumley' does the Opera—and how well ;
How 'Taste' chemiseless wander'd through the Land
Until he took her hopeless cause in hand ;
'Twill do him no small good, if we express
Opinions somewhat differing from the Press.
No 'free admission' nibs our venal pen :
He's screwed us many a time, and will again.

Well! if we pay as none e'er paid before,
The 'menue' ought to justify the score;
Nor should the Season's first three months be pass'd
In trying what 'the House' will stand at last,
By way of Operas, and vulgar ballets
Made to work up stale stock of old Swiss châlets,
And foist on us 'artistes,' whose dreadful legs
Are either thick as posts or thin as pegs:
While scraggy English Prima Donnas teach
The latent value of a native screech;
And rise so wondrous high, and sink so low,
And give our ears and temper such a blow,
As justifies the voice that longs to roar,
'Sin if thou will'st! but prithee sing no more!'
Then '*insolent St. Leons*' meet our eyes
And cause us—arch the brows in fresh surprise,
To see the Public bearded by a dancer,
And bullied in the morrow's prints for answer.
While packs of 'claqueurs' in close order plac'd
Applaud his nameless outrages on taste,
Till cramm'd with pride, and destitute of shame,
Th' uncudgell'd hound mistake the sound for fame.
Enough of him,—but, 'Lumley,' let us see
What 'tis the Public will require of thee!

Begin a little earlier next year,
To give us Singers that we long to hear!
Let 'Grisi's' matchless voice and lovely smile
Wait for no Summer to delight our Isle.
Restore us soon 'Lablache's' glorious base;
And gentle 'Persiani's' simple grace;

And, oh, restore the melody that floats
Round souls entranced by 'great Rubini's' notes!
With him, let 'exiled Tamburini' come:
And your severest critic will be dumb!

Lumley! reform!—forget awhile thyself,
And give the Public one poor chance with pelf!
But next year—prithee fear to hire again
Such rattling volleys of the venal pen!
Absurd bombast and ill-directed praise
Catch gulls no longer in these scornful days.
And though your deeds (like onions strung in ropes),
Flavour 'the Post' with 'Jenkinsonian' tropes,
Though every claqueur in the House descry
Good taste presiding o'er your mummery;
And only critics whom you can't deceive,
Who pay for boxes, stalls, and music, grieve;
Though all, and more than this result,—my Jew,
Remember! 'Taste is govern'd by the few!'

Solomon.

A NOBLE head, a loving eye,
  A figure ripe and fair,
A brow of pensive mystery,
  A comet's length of hair!
And all this wealth is mine, my Love!
  And secret treasures more
Than slaves of necromantic lamp
  In Ophir's caves explore!

The wisest King earth ever saw
  Drinks heaven at thine eyes;
Thy veriest freak his empire's law;
  And yet they call him 'Wise!'
And men call women fools, my Love,
  And so perchance they be;
But woman as thou art, my Love,
  Behold thy slave in me

Speak! and this rock at thy command
  Shall shiver to its base,
And bowing round thy throne shall stand
  The 'Jinn's' tremendous race!
They'll fetch thee gems from 'Samercand,'
  And pearls from 'Taprobane,'
A flower from 'Eden's' bless'd abodes,
  Conceal'd so long in vain.

Or doth Ambition plume thy wing,
  And empires wouldst thou sway?
My sceptre in the dust I'll fling,
  And abdicate to-day;
Content so I may dwell with thee,
  And sun me in thine eye,
Prevent thy least enduring wish,
  And love thee till I die!

They say that Eblis, when he sought
  Man's Paradise below,
And through the fair first woman wrought
  A wilderness of woe,
What time 'the fruit' smil'd in her hand,
  Did whisper in her ear
A charm no mortal can withstand,
  Nor, without yielding, hear.

And this her rich inheritance
  Descended is to thee;
I feel it in thine eye's dark glance,
  Thy voice's melody—
The music of a tuneful heart,
  That doth thy life inspire!
Ask; for whatever I can give
  Falls short of my desire.

Then, shall I speak the 'word of power,'
  And bid lost angels frame
Another 'Tadmor' in the 'Waste,'
  To celebrate thy name?

Fountains, and porches marble-arch'd,
  Ten thousand columns' shade,
Where nothing but the 'Bedoueen's' flock
  And the wild Ibex stray'd?

Or dost thou long to know the word,
  The secret of the seal,
That only I of men have heard,
  And tremble to reveal?
Though strange and mortal mine offence,
  And dire the penance be,
I'll fall, like 'Adam' with his mate,
  And brave the fiends for thee.

Friends, riches, honours! what are they?
  And this fond bauble, power?
The puppets of a summer's day,
  The playthings of an hour!
But he who loves owns everything,—
  Such glamour love hath lent,
Tho' the blest fool's sole empire be
  A camel and a tent.

Then shall I leave this palac'd rock,
  And ride forth arm'd, to roam
An 'Emir,' with a wand'ring flock,
  And the 'Desert' for his home?
Or shall I send 'my thousands' out,
  And for thy pleasure fling
Defiance in the Lion's teeth
  Of 'Assur's' furious king?

There is no wish thine heart can frame,
  Nor pageant for thine eye,
Nor marvel—give it but a name,
  And I th' event will try.
To keep thy cherish'd heart, 'my Love,'
  And watch my service bring
Fresh roses to thy kindling cheek,—
  This is to be a king.

By the Waters of Babylon.

IN the summer-tide heats, by the clear purling streams,
  Through the gardens of 'Babylon' springing,
We sat down and wept, while 'Assyrian' themes
  Strange maidens around us were singing!

The harps of our country, the harps of our pride,
  We hung on the trees where we lay;
For the music of 'Sion' remorsefully died
  In echoes of sadness away.

'Ho! maidens so famous for musical lore!
  Renown'd in all lands for your skill,
Sing us one of the songs that to gladness of yore
  Woke the mazes of Siloa's rill!'

'Shall we sing the Lord's song in the conqueror's land?
  With outcasts shall gladness agree?
No! Hush'd be the measure and palsied the hand
  When a slave strikes the harp of the free!

'For the sins of the people belov'd of the Lord
  Are many and grievous in dye;
Mute, mute is her anthem, and broken her sword,
  And her sons in captivity lie!

'And the sceptre of David, the tender, the true,
Departs in the shadows of 'Saul;'
And the tale of our griefs ye may read it anew
'Twixt yonder wing'd Bulls on the wall.'

O daughter of Babylon! soon to be torn
By misery, watching, and groans!
Bless'd, bless'd shall his hand be that makes thee forlorn,
And flings thy first-born to the stones!

Breach of Promise.

(Taken from a Newspaper Report.)

Says 'Jack,' the lawyer, to 'Tom Jones,'
The sexton call'd as witness,—
'In marriages, thou man of bones,
I do not see thy fitness.'

'Hold hard,' cries Jones, 'my lawyer lad!
Nor think you've made a merry hit;
A population must be had,
Or how am I to bury it?'

Glenshiro (pronounced Glenshero).

PART I.

1842.

CONTENTS.—The Poet laudeth some individuals and damneth others.—Compareth the length of a Highland mile with the length of the 'Honble. Col. Henry Montagu's stories.—Describeth the party, first in the general, and then in the particular.—Discourseth of Hunting.—Detaileth the start; and invoketh the Muse to commemorate the '*traps*' belonging to the party.—The episode of 'Basto.'—The anger of 'Brailsford.'—Apostrophe to the shades of 'Vatel' and 'Carême.'—*à propos* of Dinner.—The Poet reacheth a lofty flight of fancy.—Taketh a detail'd farewell of the best beats, and sweareth he will never forget them, nor the money they cost.—Sudden close of this veracious history.

Written in the year 1842, and sent to Sir William Massey Stanley, Bart., of Hooton, Cheshire. The notes added in the year 1877.

DEAR MASSEY,—

Bright was the morn, auspicious was the day,
When first to *Shiro-More* we took our way.
We pass unmoved the dingy walls of Blair,
Nor care a fig for any *Murray* there;
For who, to take his Moors would give a rap,
Or try *Glen Lyon's* courtesy—or tap?

'*Shiro-more*'—Glenshero, or Glenshiro. This moor, in 1842, extended over sixty or seventy thousand acres. It march'd with 'Lord Lovat' on the left bank of the Spey, and 'Clunie' to the fall of the watershed towards Loch Laggan. 'Corry'arraick' and 'Loch Spey' were both included within its boundaries. It was once part of the property of the Dukes of Gordon, but was sold at the same time with many of the western portions of their great estates. At this time it was rented by Sir W. M. Stanley and myself, and belong'd to Mr. Baillie.

Fellar—as far as I'm concern'd—may be
Especially well blow'd!—and so may he!
Thanks to your prudent management, we're bound
To Landlords, not such screws, and better ground.

To do your talents justice, there are few so
Fit as you to grapple with old *Cruso;*
The sly old Lawyer deevil, had you blunder'd,
Had clapp'd us on at least another 'hundred.'
Yet, render thanks to him, through whom you took
That last best French discovery, your *Cook;*
And would not let the Dundee steamer sail
Without a batch of *Hodgson's* glorious 'pale.'

Your Highland miles, though long as any two
Stories of Colonel Henry Montagu,
Still cannot last for ever—'twas the fate
Of four real trumps, who could drink wine for eight,
To muster round Glenshiro's humble board,
And rough it on such cheer as hills afford;
Folks who were fond of racing, wine, and laughter,
Could ride before they din'd, as well as after;
In every feat of manhood took their part,
And play'd the devil with a female heart.

The 'Parties' here, O well-bred Muse declare!
Nor leave the Public wond'ring who they were.

'*Hodgson's pale.*' At this date, pale ale was brew'd by 'Hodgson' of London. 'Messrs. Bass' and 'Alsop' of Burton-on-the-Trent had their reputations yet to make.

Sir William first—well vers'd in Scottish war,
Through wide *Killin*, *Loch Ericht*, and *Fellar*,
In early youth luxuriously fast,
His was the art to go the pace and last.
His was the pride, in spite of Fate's decrees
And Nature's laws, to winter on green peas.
He lov'd the Turtle, not disguis'd with flour,
And thick as fog—but clear as Summer shower,
Through whose light gauze the glorious Sunbeams play,
And give a cool transparency to day.
He lov'd, and so do I, and so do you,
Fair skin, brown hair, and eyes of speaking blue.
He lov'd—and there we're all agreed again—
Perhaps you differ?—'seven' for his main.
He lov'd when Autumn strips the rustling trees,
And dismal rain comes pattering down the breeze,
And he who knows no better longs for Spring,—
Thro' the *Launde Woods* to hear the Foxhounds ring;
Pastoral Music—prelude to the burst;
Nerves we have all—but one must needs be first.
Pink for his colour, courage for his guide,
No stile too stiff, no yawning brook too wide,
Far as his horse can go, the scent can hold,
In strong excitement vigilant, yet bold,
Behold the *Workman!* Phœbus! may I be
Ere the cold grave receive me, such as he!

Sir William Massey Stanley, of Hooton, Cheshire, 10th Baronet. He and I took the Moor together, and we each ask'd a friend,—Sir William, the Hon[ble]. James Macdonald, now Major-General; and I, Richard George Lumley, now ninth Earl of Scarborough.

Crash goes the ox-fence—slither goes the stile—
Slosh goes the brook—and weary seems each mile—
Sob goes the ridge and furrow—'twas not so,
Believe me, Reader, half an hour ago,
When first we took the *Dodger* by the head;
Dous'd our cigar;—but all his jump is fled.
Sir William was of those who scorn to do
What others try with one man, under two!
Loader, and keeper, gillies for the dogs,
And two to pull his pony out of bogs:
One for his lunch—a brace of ne'er-do-weels
To pick the birds up, and to pack the creels
In stories, like to those of old renown
In *Modern Athens'* finnan-stinking Town.
Thus did *Clan Stanley* muster for the chase,
And bag, ere evening, more than ninety brace.

'Tother your humble servant—who'd a smattering
Of most things, added to a knack of chattering
As fast as tongue could wag—the only good
I know of him—he'd stop it if he could.
His life had been an odd one—he was quiet
For one-and-twenty years, and then ran riot.
He read the Greek Philosophers—made flies—
Caught trout, and was reputed slow and wise.
Took a degree—wrote verses—fell in love—
Got into Parliament, and gave a shove
To '*Daniel the Big Beggarman,*' who star'd,
And squar'd, and star'd, and stared again and squar'd.
Soon tir'd of this—declin'd to be the serf
Of country Solons, and took up the Turf.

Made books on Derbies, Ledgers, Oaks, and Cups,
Experienc'd all the bettor's downs and ups;
Won money—spent it—lost—besieg'd the Jews,
Kind souls who rarely elder sons refuse!
Thump'd *Crockie's* board of perilous green cloth,
And strangely did not get his money's worth.
Flirted as much as did him good—'tis pleasant,
And means we are not much in love at present.
Lastly, to make his money go the faster,
Own'd *Nelly*, *Larry*, *Deuce Ace*, and the *Caster*.

How cheerful over *Garvie* peeps the day,
Not charg'd with clouds, nor treacherously gay;
Aurora wears a matron's thoughtful mien,
And drops the romping school-girl of fifteen.
'My dearest fellow! no one stirs a peg
Until he's first conceal'd another egg;
We do not lunch till two—and now 'tis seven,
And you'll be calling out about eleven.
Besides, I've vow'd that lunch shall not take place
Until we've bagg'd our five-and thirty brace!'

'*Dick*,' who in silence now some time had sat,
With head deep down in bowl of chocolate,
Rose, like a five-pound trout inclin'd to feed;—
Held out his plate—and '*Jem*' said, 'Oh! indeed!'
And now that safe in hold the eggs are put—let
Me advise just one more Red-deer cutlet!

Larry, Deuce Ace, etc., names of race-horses.

'Agreed!' cried both—'and since the meat is brown,
A glass of claret round to wash it down!'

Say, gentle Muse! how many varied traps,
Pouches, horns, luncheon-cases, copper caps;—
Or rather hold thy tongue, for fear we bore
Fastidious readers with a long dry score.
Enough that there were pointer-dogs in packs,
And long-legg'd gillies with prodigious backs,
And shelties too that bore a rude 'ephippium,'
And span-new '*Crowther*' each to flank and whip-me-em.

'Whizz—bur-r-r—slap, bang—'fore George, you've
sav'd the hashing!
Those curs'd new guns are precious hands at smashing!
Down, *Basto!* Charge!—Toho! He's got a grouse
Half down his throat as big as a small house!'
The span-new dog-whip now describes a figure
Resembling eight, and falls with healthy vigour.
The worthy beast betrays his startled feelings
By sundry tenor yells and treble squealings;
And when, at length, you think he's brought to feel
His true position, takes forthwith to heel.
'Hold up, good dog! hold up, you nasty cur!'
But de'il a bit does Basto choose to stir.

The day advances—*Brailsford* d—ns the ground,
And asks the spot where birds are mostly found;

'*Crowther.*' 'Crowther and Callow,' in Park Lane, at that time the fashionable whip-makers.

'*Brailsford.*' In after days Brailsford, and his sons, were the inaugurators of the Dog Shows, which have since become so popular.

Talks of a Moor in Yorkshire, where you fill
Your bag in half a crack, hight *Wemersgill;*
But here the grouse are fewer, and hills steeper.—
With that he damns the gillies, and the keeper,
And asks which road to take? The Celt, whose best
Performance is not English—says, 'Just West!'
O tantalizing West! it seems to me,
The Scottish compass has no point but thee;
The wind no airt; the Gael no other mode
To make a travell'r comprehend a road.

Westward we go—the grouse in larger batches—
Brailsford growls on, and licks what dogs he catches;
'Tohos!' who-whoops!—throws grouse into the air,
At which three brace of pointers all start fair.

Aurora now return'd to that old sinner
Tython's red-dressing-room—and we to dinner.

Shades of the mighty men who cook'd for fame,
Vatel the sensitive, refin'd *Carême*,
And thou, great genius gifted to produce
That touching picture of the Strasbourg goose,
Look down with nose etherealiz'd, and sniff
Fillets of grouse, and say, on honour, if
Your brightest efforts, e'en with kings to please,
Achiev'd in fancy fillets such as these!
I swear by *Ude's* atrocious *one-horse shay*,
His nankeen breeks and broad-brimm'd castor's play,

'*One-horse shay.*' Ude, the great artist, used to drive himself about in a most extraordinary vehicle of this sort.

By each 'hors d'œuvre' that *Sefton's* table grac'd,
And by our own unquestionable taste,
No 'plât' more lightly succulent e'er met
The kindling eyes of Hebrew gourmand yet.

The morn rose pregnant with disastrous news,
For half our army could not wear their shoes;
One loader cut it—and we're bound to say
That soda-water usher'd in our day.
As for the rest—at each succeeding turn
They might be seen 'doup up' in every burn.
'Tis a fine thing, that burnie's gurgling note,
And causes huskiness about the throat.

Thus day succeeded day, and slaughter, slaughter,
And each began and clos'd with soda-water.
The Cook devising dishes without number,
And pipes preparing as for well-earned slumber;
While some would snooze in easy leathern chair,
And some write nonsense to the absent fair,
And some admire their kilts—for kilts we wore,
And voted patent 'keyseymeres' a bore.—
Oh, happy days! by no reflection cross'd
(Except the little fortune that ye cost);
Oh, happy days! when years shall add their weight
To these fleet limbs, and whiten this black pate,—
When idle youth, irreverently bold,
Shall dub us bores, and, still worse, call us old;
Still may this heart, undimm'd by selfish age,
Glow as of yore with friendship's noble rage,
And Memory gilding scenes too bright to last,
Cast her bright halo round the chequer'd past:

Still may I love the rude unculturd ground
Where simple hearts and vig'rous hands abound,
Where you and I have rang'd the mountain side,
Health our pursuit, and noble game our guide;
With cheek embrown'd, and vigour in each limb,—
Man is a splendid creature, when in trim!

Farewell to *Garvie Wood*, and *Laggan's* shore!
To *Corry-Arraick* I return no more.
Unharm'd by me the silly grouse may stray
From *Clunie's* march to thy far banks, *Loch Spey!*
Adieu, *Black Corry! Parson's Beat* farewell!
To happier wights belong the charms I tell.
I can't afford to take your glories on,—
For half their zest and all my money's gone!
Yet oft shall Memory's faithful glance retrace,
In after days, the humours of the place.
Tom Taylor's flaming face in dreams shall rise,
And younger *Brailsford's* disappearing eyes,
Brailsford himself come shuffling down the stairs
With foot in shot-bag, and eyes scarcely pairs;
Once more along the hills his shouts shall peal,
And *Basto* duly thrash'd shall slink to heel.
Johnny, and *Fife*, the picture here shall grace,
And *Vara-Pitie* with his rueful face.
Life has not many happier days in store,
Than those we shot away at *Garvie More!*

'*Johnny*.' 'Johnny' and 'Vara-Pitie' were gillies. The latter had little or no English, so he contented himself with replying indifferently to all questions in the phrase, 'It's vara pitie.' I once saved him from dismissal at a heavy price; for, out of gratitude, he ever afterwards attached himself to me. 'Fife' was the keeper belonging to the moor.

Glenshiro.

PART II.

1843.

DEAR MASSEY,—
Alas ! how changeable is life ! Last year
We batter'd down the grouse and slew the deer,
Swore at the corns that interfer'd with walking,
And bless'd the fools that would not give us stalking ;
While episodical accounts went round
Of all the grouse we kill'd, and all we found,
And all we did, and all we would have done.
Hills of Glenshiro ! theatres of fun !
Must I be doom'd in London town to fret,
And leave your joys to scribble in a pet ?
Is there no pensive Jew with soul to lend ?
No millionaire Motteux to stand my friend ?
Oh, Cotherstone ! thou curs'd of Heaven's decree,
Dear as a 'two-year-old' wast thou to me !
Dear as a 'three !' and still more when my purse
Has seen thee win 'the Leger,' and my curse.
Hadst thou been early nobbled, lam'd, or roasted,
Of full four thousand pounds it now had boasted !
Four thousand arguments against dull sorrow,
Four thousand reasons to forget the morrow,
Four thousand cubits added to the three
That now our stature seems to men to be.

But since invidious Fate rejects my prayer
For whisky, grouse, pale ale, and mountain air;
Since now no more my failing limbs I drag
Up the steep brae where points the villain '*Brag*;'
(*A propos* of the baste, I trust your log
Contains approving notice of the dog;)
Since now no more in flowing kilt array'd
I struggle with the wind that twists my plaid;
I still behold in Memory's faithful glass
(As Surrey did of old) the figures pass
Of 'Taylor,' 'Vara-Pitie,' 'Brailsford,' 'Fife,'
And the 'Clan Stanley,' clad for mountain strife;
Lastly, a vision of the She 'Mac-Nab,'
Proud of her wreath of flowers, and gift of gab.
Of stately port a London lady she,
Of gorgeous manners and of high degree.
Ere 'Mac' transferr'd her to the land o' grouse,
She and her sister kept a lodging-house,
So now she rules with conscious air of queen
That knows what manners and deportment mean.

But let's to business! Since you left the city
Some have done foolish things, and some said witty.
'Ceritos' danced exactly one foot higher
Than 'Fanny Elssler;' by the Queen's desire
'*Adolphus*' is to boil the royal kettle
As far as Portsmouth. Like a lad of mettle,

'*Brag.*' A first-rate pointer which I lent to Sir William Massey Stanley, to whom this letter was sent.

'*Adolphus.*' Lord Adolphus FitzClarence, Captain of the first 'Royal Yacht.'

They say he grumbled when he saw the space
Allotted to the footmen—scant o' grace
But large o' beam—while all the loyal sailors
Were stowed away on little boards, like tailors.
'Tis said another Deluge may be dreaded,
So many couples here have pair'd and wedded,
And gone into the matrimonial ark ;—
Some for true love, and others for a lark.
Indeed I may affirm, while on this topic,
That ladies ne'er were known more philanthropic ;
At least, I never knew them in my day
So prompt to cherish, honour, and obey.

By this time you'll be conscious at Glenshiro,
That English beef and ale feed 'Espartero.'
He landed some days since ; with him another
Heroic wight, who piked Cabrera's mother,
And several other Dons, who think it funny
To pay no interest upon English money.
'Peel' being asked to tell us what he was,
Said, 'He's 'de jure' Regent still—that's poz !
But not 'de facto,' or he'd not be here !'
This explanation's statesmanlike and clear.
With soul for several reasons cross and huffy,
And weather preternaturally stuffy,
It is not good to stew in town. Arouse,
Obedient Muse, and sing a lay of Cowes !

Cowes boasts an inconvenient town ; it's cove
Is fit for mooring yachts and making love ;
Its produce widows, prawns, and telescopes ;
Its prospects ropes and masts, and masts and ropes ;

Its conversation nautical; its wrangling
As hard to cure as squinting, love, or gambling.
But still I'm somehow restless in a yacht,
And never yet slept sound in any cot.
I hate the pitching of your heavy seas,
And don't appreciate a 'commanding breeze.'

Now to ask questions since I've told some news:—
How many of your army still wear shoes?
How fares it with the '*Colonel*,' '*Lad*,' *and* '*Ches?*'
I trust they toddle in the 'Hieland dress.'
What is your daily draught on 'Hodgson's pale?'
At what o'clock does luncheon most prevail?
Are your whole party well aware 'tis silly
To shoot a pointer or blaspheme a gilly?
How goes the 'Leger' betting? After dinner,
Which horse in your opinion's mostly winner?
How do the fair describe their widowed state?
Do they submit and sigh, or compensate?

So now, farewell! by Fortune forc'd to change,
For me no moors expand, no pointers range.
Like every other dog I've had my day:
My occupation's now to see the play,
And watch the parts, or lash in scornful rhymes
The ninnies and the follies of our times.
A few years since, good-natur'd to a fault,
I almost fear'd to sprinkle too much salt;
Now, older grown and taught to measure men,
I dip in gall an irritable pen.

'*The Colonel*,' 'Col. the Hon. George Anson.' '*The Lad*,' 'The Hon. Henry Forester,' and 'The Earl of Chesterfield.'

The Choice of a Commodore.

AUGUST, 1847.

WHEN Time took Lord Yarborough down by the stern,
And the *Kestrel* returned with the Commodore's urn,
There was mourning at Cowes, lamentation at Ryde,
For the jolly old tar was the whole island's pride.

He was bluff in his bearings, and broad in his beam;
The Club was his child and its doings his theme;
He had seen it grow up, he had foster'd it well,
And delivered it sound to the guidance of 'Bel.'

Ere the fun'ral was over the wrangling began,
On the much-approved Royal Cowes Yacht Squadron plan.
Some wanted a sailor, some wanted a duke,
Some wanted a Commodore with a good cook.

Some spoke of Lord Wilton, and some of 'Lord Bel.'
Some thought that the '*Marquis*' would do quite as well.
Some talked of themselves and their nautical feats,
For your 'Nab-going Nelsons' are positive treats.

F. M. the first Marquis of Anglesey.

Some backed and some filled, and some stay'd, and some
  wore,
Some stood out to sea, and some sniggled in shore;
Some said, 'If he give up, the sooner the better;'
Some twiddled their thumbs, and some talked of 'a letter.'

Then out spoke George Bentinck, so bluff and so bold,—
'The yarn I shall spin you is very soon told.
You may choose him indeed, but he won't do for me!
He may suit Hyde Park Corner, but I'm off to sea.'

'Magregor's' or Mac-Gregory's Gathering.

A NEW VERSION, AS SUNG BY 'STUNNING JOE' AND CHORUS.

WRITTEN ABOUT THE YEAR 1843.

PAY! pay! you must all of you pay,
Or your names will be down in his Paper next day!
Pay 'ten' or 'twenty,'
If money be plenty.
Pay him in bank-notes at the first summons.
Quick! lest you be too late;
'*Gregory's nod*' is fate!
Pay through your noses, gentles and commons!

Gregory's nod. An unscrupulous rogue of the name of 'Gregory' was the Editor and Proprietor of the *Satirist*, one of the most abominable papers by which the literature of any country has ever been defil'd. He converted it into a secret machinery for obtaining money under threats, and in some instances pocketed incredibly large sums to insure his silence. At last he fell, brought to justice and confusion in the way he least expected. The ex-Duke of Brunswick filed a criminal information against him for libels published in the *Satirist*, and after conducting the case in person, succeeded in getting a verdict, which entailed upon the rascal an imprisonment of two years' duration. His paper was ruin'd, he himself was reduced to poverty, and I rather think he died in jail before the term of his sentence had expired. His miserable fate, however, has not proved a sufficient warning to the 'Pasquins' of this age.

Down with your names as '*Shakespearians*,' down with them!
Swear that your master is greater than 'Kemble,' and
'Kean' and 'Macready,'
And good Doctor Eady!
Down on your marrow-bones all of you! tremble and
Pay, pay! &c. &c.

Pay! lest the servants' hall echo with ribaldry!
Pay! lest the 'public-house' laugh at your daughters!
Pay! lest a friend relate
All your bad jokes of late!
'Crocky's' has spies, and 'White's' its reporters.
So pay, &c. &c.

Pay! pay! you need none of you pay!
For, who cares a fig for 'the Paper' to-day?
'Talfourd' has trounced the rogue,
Libels are not in vogue,
Scandal is silenced, lies are a dead letter!
Shut up shop, Gregory!
Lest you and beggary
Shake hands in jail; and the sooner the better!
Pay! pay! you need none of you pay!

'*Shakespearians.*' Under the mask of subscriptions to the 'Shakespearians,' a club of private theatricals got up by 'Gregory,' the 'black-mail' was levied. I one day received a letter inviting me to belong to it; to which I returned for answer that 'I could take care of myself, and begged to defy Mr. Gregory and all his works.' I heard no more of the matter, neither was I attacked in the newspaper.

A Chaunt

ANENT THE DOINGS OF THE 'NEWMARKETS AND CHESTERFORDS.'

'BELL'S LIFE,' 1851.

SINCE we first brought out our line,
About 'eighteen thirty-nine,'
In that snuggest of localities, 'Stag Alley,'
We've had calls at least a score,
But the more they paid, the more
The 'Chesterfords' went dropping down in 'valley;'

Till we'd call'd up every cent;
And what's more, it was all spent
In a fashionable station with Greek columns:
They were *à propos* enough,
For we 'Greek'd' 'em pretty rough,
And the shareholders were smitten with 'the solemns.'

So, to keep in decent bounds,
We had sixty thousand pounds
Of rolling-stock upon our ten-mile line;
Oh, how moderate we were!
How ridiculously fair!
'Hudson' envied us our plant, it was so fine.

Soon, to get a little money,
We mortgaged it—how funny!
For twenty in the hundred, to a Jew;
Who sold it up next year:
When the shareholders, we hear,
Had the impudence to talk about a 'do.'

But a Company's a farce!
So of course we gave it 'sarce.'
For your shareholders are really such poor creatures
That, betwixt us, brothers all,
Excepting for a 'call,'
One never cares to see their ugly features.

At last came out our smash,
And the Chesterfords went crash,
From 'twenty-three pounds paid' to ten poor 'bob.'
And among the other bounties
Of the glorious 'Eastern Counties'
They taught us irresponsibly to rob.

For they worked our line a year,
And then said,—'It was quite clear
That they never had sign'd anything to bind!
They'd lost money for their parts,
And, God bless our foolish hearts!
They'd the best of grounds for altering their mind!'

So of course we need not mention
That we got up an 'extension'
To Bury, that great market-place for seeds;

That kept us on a year!
For we soon shall make it clear
  How famously a line of that sort bleeds.

Cock-and-bullish tales invent,
Promise interest—five per cent!
  Put down nest-egg names, a hundred men of straw!
Then, if you're a cunning file
You will let it stand awhile,
  For, as sure as stags wear horns, that 'goak' will draw.

And you cannot choose but win,
When the public rushes in
  With its dirty ten-pound notes for deposit:
Spend the one half in your bill,
Put the t'other in your till,
  And see the 'green-horns' gull'd from your closet!

Then, after four long years
Take out your office shears,
  And cut your liabilities full snip;
And offer them all round,
Three shillings in the pound,
  To sign you a surrender of their scrip.

Most took it with a grunt,
For few turn away 'the blunt'
  When it's ready, and the needful meets the eye.
But others filed a Bill,
And put us in the mill
  Of Chanc'ry, where it's now in pound we lie.

So of course we cut a dash,
And settled the fools' hash
  By looking up the 'shareholders' forthwith,
And registering all;—
Of which move, a 'three-pound call,'
  Is, brothers, as you're well aware, the pith.

So, with or without funnel,
Let us make out little tunnel!
  For our rigging little railroad up to Bury.
Though the Jockey Club may thunder,
We'll go over, or go under
  The Warren Hill;—then, railway stags, be merry!

For all the money subscribed, there remains nothing to show but the Station with the Greek columns, and certain ruinous heaps between the termini, reminding one of the prophetic curse upon Babylon.

The Grey-lag Goose.

WRITTEN AT BERKELEY CASTLE, DEC. 23. 1874.

THE grey-lag goose is a gentle fowl.
He feeds where it suits his whim ;
On the broad grass mead you may see him indeed,
But how will you master him ?

Gaggle—gaggle—gaggle, goes the good grey goose ;
You'll hear his note resound,
As you lie in rank under Severn's bank,
From all the meadows round,

Or snug at the edge of the blackthorn hedge,
In friendly ditch conceal'd :
Keep close till he flies, with a *roaring rise*,
From the hundred-acre field !

'*A roaring rise.*' In the meadows of the Severn, about four miles from Berkeley Castle, there are at times in a good year, and severe weather, from fifteen hundred to two thousand of the grey-lag goose to be seen feeding. After the guns are plac'd, the drivers disturb the flock ; when it rises with the sound of distant thunder, and the birds seek the banks and ooze of the estuary of the Severn. They remain there usually long enough to allow of a good lunch for the sportsmen ; after which, should the weather be favourable—or, in other words, a mixture of snow, sleet, and fog—they begin to return by small detachments to their old feeding-ground. The guns have by this time lin'd the bank of the Severn ; and as the birds often fly low over it, the best shooting begins. Large bags are occasionally made, but half-a-dozen wild geese make a

His home is afar, beneath the North Star,
  In the 'Lapman's' dismal land:
But he flits betimes to milder climes,
  And Severn's favoured strand.

And there in the maze of her ooze he plays,
  Far from the murd'rous shore;
Till on hungry wings aloft he springs,
  And trusts the meads once more.

Let the first go by, be he ne'er so nigh,
  And, faith! they're drawing near!
For the kindly note of wings and throat,
  Makes music loud and clear.

The grey-lag goose is a gentle fowl;
  He feeds where it suits his whim:
But '*long Tom Sayers*' took him unawares;—
  And so thou hast master'd him.

---

very respectable show; and it should be recollected that these 'Berkeley' meadows are the only ground in England where the birds may be regularly expected, and 'goosing,' as it is call'd, forms one of the establish'd sports of the Castle.

'*Long Tom Sayers.*' As the geese fly high it is the custom to use large guns, with a charge very often purposely exaggerated. These guns have all got names. One in particular being nam'd after the indomitable champion of the ring. This well-known implement usually behaves more unkindly to the sportsman who has the management of it than it does to the geese. After loosing off 'Tom Sayers,' it is not unusual for the stranger who assists for the first time at the sport of 'goosing' to find himself lying on his back, with his collar-bone more or less broken, and the goose well on towards the horizon.

Whalley.

JANUARY 24, 1874.

Tune—'Hey, Johnny Cope!'

'WHALLEY' arose from dreams of night,
He tweak'd his nose and found it right,
For he was full of frolic and fight,
As an Irish lad i' the morning.

Says he, 'I'll strike opponents dumb,
With my rattling, roaring memorandum:
What care I for the "fee-fo-fum"
Of Judges, or "Skipworth's" warning?'

'I've got a tale will make 'em scatter,
And shame the "de'il" in a certain matter:
And where's the man that dares to patter,
When Whalley awakes i' the morning?'

So off he set, for his wig lay handy,
And much he fancied his '*copia fandi;*'
But they said, 'He had no "*locus standi,*"'
To tell his tale i' the morning.

'Beshrew my heart! the Pope is here!
He's flavour'd all our beef and beer!
And now he sits i' the bench, I fear!
In the shape of "beak" i' the morning!'

So down he went to Peterbro',
As fast as express train could go,
And, spite of the Judges—that 'terrible show,'—
He writ to the *Times* i' the morning.

And such a shock as he drew down
Upon his testifying crown,
Clean beggar'd that of old renown
Which Franklin got i' the morning.

For tipstaff's hand compulsion laid
Upon his stainless shoulder-blade,
And none could bring efficient aid,
Till fine was paid by sister.

Oh, woman! when we make a fool
Of our great selves (a common rule!),
Thou hast the gift to drive a mule!
And, 'faith, he would have miss'd her!

For next day came 'the Premier's' missile,
Or, sooth to say, his 'Greenwich Epistle;'
Which caused M.P.'s to fret and whistle,
And call bad names i' the morning.

And who is he makes bold to say,
If 'Whalley' were in 'Holloway,'
'His lambs' might not be off, and stray
To other folds i' the morning?

Change for a Pound.

COLONEL George Tomline, a short time ago,
Sent a pound of gold to his friend 'Bob Lowe.'
For says he—'To my workmen their wages I owe,
And there ain't a 'mag of silver' to be had, 'Bob Lowe.'
So coin away florins very fast, you know!
Deliver us the dollars, my Magnifico!
You're bound to change a pound into pieces white and round,
Which cannot now be found anywhere, 'Bob Lowe!''

Robert look'd up and he cried—'What, ho!'
Which prettily express'd that it was 'no go!'
And says he—'To blue-blazes' the world may blow.
Victoriæ anno quinto trigesimo,
If ever you get change out of 'Robert Lowe,'
Though with milk and honey your tongue should flow;
Which is just as like as reason in a 'strike,'
Or a pig to keep a 'pike,'—or a live 'Dodo.''

'But I've law on my side, my old friend 'Bob Lowe!'
And I've 'jaw' beside, at which you're not slow.
My lawyer tells me this, and he's bound to know.
So be ready with the 'shiners,' my soft-tongued 'Bob Lowe.'
I'll trouble you for florins, my good milk-white crow.
'Couters,' and 'benders,' and 'joeys' also.
And Bobby, from your lobby, since it is my hobby,
Without my change in silver I will never go.'

Then the Judges declar'd, sitting all on a row,
Blinking in their wigs in the full 'banco;'
'There was no compulsion upon 'Robert Lowe.''
But let's all sing heigh! and let's all sing 'ho!'
For after beating the Colonel and Co.,
And giving them 'con,' when they look'd for 'pro,'
He's swallow'd down the pill of his own free will,
And coin'd us twenty millions, has our 'Robert Lowe.'

‘Ex Luce lucellum.’

NEW MOTTO FOR A MATCH-BOX, BY THE RIGHT HONBLE. ROBERT LOWE

APRIL 26.

WE are told there is joy when one naughty boy
Repenteth;
And now there'll be *no more processions*,—for Lowe
Relenteth.

The match-trade, undone for the sake of a pun,
Recovers;
And now in the ‘lobby’ they look out for Bobby
Like lovers.

But if I might offer to such a prime scoffer
Opinions;
Dear Bob! you'll set right your loss upon light,
Off ‘chignons.’

‘*No more processions.*’ The Chancellor of the Exchequer was at last obliged to give up both his crotchet and his pun, by a procession of all the lucifer-match makers and their friends, which arriv'd at the doors of the Palace of Westminster to petition Parliament on the subject.

The pun, ‘A small profit off light,’ was of a most ‘ancient and fish-like flavour.’

The Swallows.

COME back with the swallows, my dearest,
Come back with the swallows in spring,
When the bird sings the loudest and clearest,
And love is in everything.

When the steed in his pastures is neighing,
The sap bursts in fronds from the tree,
And the maids they are all gone a-maying,
Come back with the swallows to me.

Jerusalem versus Balham.

1876.

IN the days of 'The Master,' 'tis very well known,
None so sinless was found as to cast the first stone;
They went out one by one, and they left Him alone.

Then said He to the woman (none else standing by),
'Where are these thine accusers? departed?—and why?
'Hath no man condemn'd thee? Then neither do I.

'Go, and sin thou no more!' But had Balham been there,
With its 'coroner's law' and Pecksniffian air,
And its foregone conclusions, loose, rash, and unfair,

With a parcel of lawyers that never agree,
Save in damaging truth in return for a fee;
Instead of 'at one,' they'd have cast stones at three.

Lawyers' Quotations.

JULY 24, 1874.

'What can ennoble fools, or knaves, or cowards?
No! not all the blood of all the Howards?'—DOCTOR KENEALY.

SAYS 'Chief Justice Cockburn' to 'Doctor Kenealy,'
If you say 'That's Pope!' you say what it ain't really!
Says 'Kenealy' to 'Cockburn,' If you say 'That's Byron!'
Your lordship's correction won't wash and won't iron!
On referring 'to Cocker' it turns out, in troth,
A bit of 'prime fustian,' the bantling of both.

MORAL.

How strange that a couplet so full of clap-trap,
Nigh as old as the hills, and as pithless as pap,
Should crop up 'twixt lawyers so learnèd and long,
And that both should be right, and both should be wrong!

The passage in Pope runs thus:—

'Go! and pretend your family is young;
Nor own your fathers have been fools so long.
What can ennoble sots, or slaves, or cowards?
Alas! not all the blood of all the 'Howards.''
POPE'S *Essay on Man*, Epistle 4, line 215.

'Doctor Kenealy' made the second line halt by half a foot when he said, 'No! not,' &c. &c.; but the 'Chief Justice,' in taking him to task, show'd that his ear was right and his memory wrong. He was 'all abroad' when he attributed the couplet to 'Byron.'

Time brings Redress.

THIRTY-FOUR cent'ries since,
During 'Pharaoh's' evictions,
We are told, 'twas a stranger
That spoil'd the Egyptians.

But the gentle 'Khedive'
Has dispos'd of this danger,
Showing how the Egyptians
Can now spoil the 'stranger.'

Thus, losers in either case
Found to their sorrow,
The process describ'd
By the little word '*borrow.*'

'*Borrow.*' 'And the children of Israel did according to the word of Moses: and they borrow'd of the Egyptians jewels of silver, and jewels of gold, and raiment.'—*Exod.* xii. 35.

'We will Die with our Husbands!'

1861.

'We will die with our husbands!' How sad was the word,
That while England lay sleeping at Cawnpore was heard!
Each head on the breast of our helpmates reclin'd,—
'We will die with our husbands! dark devils of Ind!'

But, alas for the story! alas for the woe!
By the bright name of Honour it might not be so!
The man to the shambles dishonour'd in dust,
The wife to the chambers of rapine and lust!

On the throne of Thy glory remember it, Lord!
Just Judge of the Balance, stern God of the Sword!
Of the sins of past empire assoil us, we pray,
While yet there are women and children to slay!

And oh! when the banners of victory meet,
On the last ruin'd tower of Nana's retreat,
And the man-eating tiger is track'd to his den,
By the hunters of England, remember it then!

The Drying-up of the great River Euphrates.

'Morning Post,' July 22, 1876.

They are coming! They are coming!
They are now upon the tread,
The 'times' of which friend '*Cumming*'
Has very often said,—
'That Abaddon's private signal-flag
Is certainly unfurl'd,
And everything's betokening
The finish of the world.'

'Twas *stock-jobbing begun the war!*
And wherefore should it not,
When 'a Bear' will boil his mother,
Wife and children, in one pot?
What matters Europe's self unseam'd,
With heaps of dead and dying,
So long as we, the 'hungry Bears,'
Send all the 'funds' a-flying?

'*Friend Cumming.*' A Rev. Gentleman who has predicted the 'finish of the world' some score of times during the last forty years.

'*Stock-jobbing begun the war.*' At the beginning, the Servian war was doubtless the handiwork of the 'Bears' on 'Change.

They were foul, they were crookèd,
  They could hardly have been scurvier,
The diplomatic dodges that
  Made a fool of Servia !
Now 'twas 'piano,' now 'andante,'
  And at odd times 'allegro;'
Some folks put faith in 'Russia,'
  And some in Monte-Negro.

But the Turks don't fly so lightly
  As their 'Six per cents' have flown !
This 'Milan,' the Prince so sprightly,
  Is likely soon to own ;
Though Cossack wits have schem'd a plan
  With promptings on the sly,
To swallow up the Bosphorus,
  And drain th' Euphrates dry.

The first thing, that of 'drying up,'
  In certain accents speaks,
Was the laying down of railroads,
  And putting Turks in breeks ;
Then the masterful predominance
  Of England's '*great Elchee*,'
Who plac'd 'the Porte' in leading strings,
  And burk'd autonomy.

'*England's great Elchee.*' By this style and title it pleases Mr. Kinglake to designate 'Lord Stratford de Redcliffe,' but he, 'Lord Stratford,' has much to answer for in being the first to put the 'Porte in leading-strings;' a system which, under a less vigorous exercise of England's will, the Russian diplomatists were quick to follow.

Where are the hundred nations
  That history describes,
Who sent the Caliph tribute
  And the swords of hardy tribes?
From Araby, the parent hive,
  To the 'Vegas' of old Spain,
And all the North of 'Afric,'
  Mother of flocks and grain.

From 'Bactria' and 'Turkestan,'
  And the much-ravag'd plains
Where 'Tigris' and 'Euphrates' shroud
  Assyria's gaunt remains;
'Damascus,' that old city
  When Abraham was young,
And 'Shushan,' the king's palace,
  Where 'Haman' high was hung.

From Afghanistan's mountain-throne,
  And 'Helmund's' glassy wave,
Where sturdy 'Rustam' erst was wont
  His boyish limbs to lave.
'Egypt,' the land of mystery,
  And longings unsuffic'd,
'*El Kuds*,' the sacred city
  Of David, and of Christ.

From the sea-board of Palestine,
  That launch'd the first marine,
'Armenia' and 'Kurdistan,'
  And all that lies between

'*El Kuds*.' A name probably taken from the word 'Cadytis,' by which Jerusalem was known in the days of Alexander.

'Pontus,' and those fair cities,
  Rich once, now lean and wan;
Up to the passage where, they say,
  Europa's voyage began.

With all that Euxine circuit,
  That, ere the birth of Greece,
The robber 'Jason' wander'd o'er,
  To snatch the golden fleece.
'Illyria,' 'Thrace,' 'Epirus,'
  And Alexander's land,
Rent by the sword of 'Mahmoud'
  From the Greek Emperor's hand.

How powerless was then the Cross!
  High names could nought avail
Against the 'Camel-driver's' men,
  Under the 'Crescent' pale.
Then, bent beneath the Moslem arm,
  So ruthless and so strong,
The land of all the Muses,
  Long time to suffer wrong.

With every isle that Mem'ry loves,
  And the chief names that claim,
On hist'ry's splendid muster-roll,
  Bright and eternal fame,—
'Thebes,' 'Athens,' 'Corinth,' 'Sparta,'
  'Rhodes,' 'Cyprus,' 'Melos,' 'Crete;'
And stolid 'Dulness' held her court
  E'en at 'Athena's' feet

Greece was, it seems, the first to part ;
But whether this was wise,
Let those declare who manag'd
'The *Navarin surprise.*'
'Untoward' was the word applied
To that sad victory,
When 'Russia' first in earnest sought
To drain th' 'Euphrates' dry.

Then came a war that ruin'd quite
The luckless Turks' affairs,
When '*Diebitch*' treated with the Porte
At the 'Blood-drinker's' stairs ;
And 'Araby' threw off the yoke,
And 'Egypt' turn'd to go,
And many a rivulet dried up,
And many a stream ran low.

'*The Navarin surprise.*' England was upon this occasion undoubtedly made to do Russia's work.

'*Diebitch.*' Marshal Diebitch, call'd 'Zabalkansky,' or 'Transcender of the Balkans.' He dictated terms to the Porte in the treaty of 'Hunkiar Skelessi,' or the Blood-drinker's stairs. 'Blood-drinker' was one of the many ornamental titles lavish'd on the Caliphs, or 'Lieutenants of the Prophet.'

There is certainly something very remarkable in the close application of the word 'drying up' to the course of events in Turkey. She is not conquer'd and subdued into the inheritance of any one conqueror, such as 'Mahmoud,' who took Byzantium, and whose descendants have held it more or less since ; but everybody takes a bit, under some plea or other, and the consequence is, as may be expected, a progressive drying up of the great river.

Till the strong river of the East,
'Euphrates,' the great flood
That roll'd so long, impetuous,
And hard to be withstood,
No longer bound within its banks,
Nor master, as of yore,
Loses itself in fen and reeds,—
And breasts the sea no more.

Cincinnatus.

August 6, 1878.

Simple manners, simple men;
'Cincinnatus' ploughs again!
Widely known for prudent lore,
He had made his mark before,
On the 'fasti' of his time;
Single-hearted and sublime.
Widely known for happy hand
On the bâton of command,
He was still the first to see
Wherein lay the mastery.
None, not even feeble friends,
Could divert him from his ends.
He could keep a secret, too!
He could plan, and he could do.

Came a day when sudden heats,
Bred of diplomatic feats;
Crazy states, and greedy kings
(Praising God above all things),
Thought to do his country wrong;
Treason throve, and lies wax'd strong.

Swords were red from points to hilts;
So they took him from the stilts,
Saying,—'Rome hath need of thee;
Craves a man, and thou art he!'

Soon before them all he stands,
With the balance in his hands.
Roman courage, Roman word,
Back'd up by a Roman's sword.
Diplomatic tricks fell through;
Justice trimm'd her scales anew.
In despite of years and health,
He hath sav'd the Commonwealth
From false friends and secret foes:
Now again he seeks repose.

Roman, thou may'st take thine ease,
Having store of sons like these.

END OF VOL. I.

LONDON:
Marcus Ward and Co., 67, 68, Chandos Street, W.C.

www.ingramcontent.com/pod-product-compliance
Lightning Source LLC
Chambersburg PA
CBHW030822270326
41928CB00007B/852

* 9 7 8 3 7 4 4 7 5 2 9 1 6 *